Blackstone's
Police Q&A

Evidence and Procedure 2024

CW01496939

Blackstone's
Police Q&A

Evidence and Procedure 2024

Twenty-second edition

Jo Lawry

Great Clarendon Street, Oxford, OX2 6DP,
United Kingdom

Oxford University Press is a department of the University of Oxford.
It furthers the University's objective of excellence in research, scholarship,
and education by publishing worldwide. Oxford is a registered trade mark of
Oxford University Press in the UK and in certain other countries

© Jo Lawry 2023

The moral rights of the author have been asserted

First Edition published in 2023

All rights reserved. No part of this publication may be reproduced, stored in
a retrieval system, or transmitted, in any form or by any means, without the
prior permission in writing of Oxford University Press, or as expressly permitted
by law, by licence or under terms agreed with the appropriate reprographics
rights organization. Enquiries concerning reproduction outside the scope of the
above should be sent to the Rights Department, Oxford University Press, at the
address above

You must not circulate this work in any other form
and you must impose this same condition on any acquirer

Public sector information reproduced under Open Government Licence v3.0
(http://www.nationalarchives.gov.uk/doc/open-government-licence/open-government-licence.htm)

Published in the United States of America by Oxford University Press
198 Madison Avenue, New York, NY 10016, United States of America

British Library Cataloguing in Publication Data
Data available

ISBN 978-0-19-889031-7

DOI: 10.1093/law/9780198890317.001.0001

Printed and bound by
CPI Group (UK) Ltd, Croydon, CR0 4YY

Links to third party websites are provided by Oxford in good faith and
for information only. Oxford disclaims any responsibility for the materials
contained in any third party website referenced in this work.

Contents

Introduction		vii
Blackstone's Police Q&As—Special Features		ix
Acknowledgements		xi
1	**Instituting Criminal Proceedings**	**1**
	Questions	1
	Answers	6
2	**Release of Person Arrested**	**11**
	Questions	11
	Answers	23
3	**Court Procedure and Witnesses**	**36**
	Questions	36
	Answers	43
4	**Exclusion of Admissible Evidence**	**49**
	Questions	49
	Answers	55
5	**Disclosure of Evidence**	**61**
	Questions	61
	Answers	68
6	**Detention and Treatment of Persons by Police Officers**	**75**
	Questions	75
	Answers	94

Contents

7   Identification   **112**

Questions   112
Answers   122

8   Interviews   **132**

Questions   132
Answers   143

Question Checklist   155

Introduction

Before you get into the detail of this book, there are two myths about multiple-choice questions (MCQs) that we need to get out of the way right at the start:

1. that they are easy to answer;
2. that they are easy to write.

Take one look at a professionally designed and properly developed exam paper, such as those used by the Police Promotion Examinations Board, and the first myth collapses straight away. Contrary to what some people believe, MCQs are not an easy solution for examiners and not a 'multiple-guess' soft option for examinees.

That is not to say that all MCQs are taxing, or even testing—in the psychometric sense. If MCQs are to have any real value at all, they need to be carefully designed and follow some agreed basic rules.

And this leads us to myth number 2.

It is widely assumed by many people and educational organisations that anyone with the knowledge of a subject can write MCQs. You need only look at how few MCQ writing courses are offered by training providers in the UK to see just how far this myth is believed. Similarly, you need only to have a go at a few badly designed MCQs to realise that it is a myth nonetheless. Writing bad MCQs is easy; writing good ones is no easier than answering them!

As with many things, the design of MCQs benefits considerably from time, training and experience. Many MCQ writers fall easily and often unwittingly into the trap of making their questions too hard, too easy or too obscure, or completely different from the type of question that you will eventually encounter in your own particular exam. Others seem to use the MCQ as a way to catch people out or to show how smart they, the authors, are (or think they are).

There are several purposes for which MCQs are very useful. The first is in producing a reliable, valid and fair test of knowledge and understanding across a wide range of subject matter. Another is an aid to study, preparation and revision for such examinations and tests. The differences in objective mean that there are slight differences in the rules that the MCQ writers follow. Whereas the design of fully validated MCQs to be used in high-stakes examinations which will effectively determine who passes and who fails have very strict guidelines as to construction, content and style, less stringent rules apply to MCQs that are being used for teaching and revision. For that reason, there may be types of MCQ that are appropriate in the latter setting which would not be used in the former. However, in developing the MCQs for this book, the author has tried to follow the fundamental rules of MCQ design but would not claim to have replicated the level of psychometric rigour that is—and has to be—adopted by the type of examining bodies referred to previously.

These MCQs are designed to reinforce your knowledge and understanding, to highlight any gaps or weaknesses in that knowledge and understanding and to help focus your revision of the relevant topics.

I hope that aim has been achieved.

Good luck!

Blackstone's Police Q&As—Special Features

References to Blackstone's Police Manuals

Every answer is followed by a paragraph reference to Blackstone's Police Manuals. This means that once you have attempted a question and looked at an answer, the Manual can immediately be referred to for help and clarification.

Unique numbers for each question

Each question and answer has the same unique number. This should ensure that there is no confusion as to which question is linked to which answer. For example, Question 2.1 is linked to Answer 2.1.

Checklists

The checklists are designed to help you keep track of your progress when answering the multiple-choice questions. If you fill in the checklist after attempting a question, you will be able to check how many you got right on the first attempt and will know immediately which questions need to be revisited a second time. Please visit www. blackstonespoliceservice.com and click through to the Blackstone's Police Q&As 2024 page. You will then find electronic versions of the checklists to download and print out. Email any queries or comments on the book to: police@oup.com.

Acknowledgements

This book has been written as an accompaniment to Blackstone's Police Manuals, and will test the knowledge you have accrued through reading that series. It is of the essence that full study of the relevant chapters in each Police Manual is completed prior to attempting the Questions and Answers. As qualified police trainers, we recognise that students tend to answer questions incorrectly either because they don't read the question properly, or because one of the 'distracters' has done its work. The distracter is one of the three incorrect answers in an MCQ, and is designed to distract you from the correct answer, and in this way discriminate between candidates: the better-prepared candidate not being 'distracted'.

So particular attention should be paid to the *Answers* sections and students should ask themselves, 'Why did I get that question wrong?' and, just as importantly, 'Why did I get that question right?' Combining the information gained in the *Answers* section together with re-reading the chapter in the Police Manuals should lead to a greater understanding of the subject matter.

The publisher and the author wish to thank Huw Smart and John Watson for their contributions to previous editions of this book.

1 Instituting Criminal Proceedings

QUESTIONS

Question 1.1

Student Police Officer, PC JOSEY, is preparing her first advice case file for consideration by the Crown Prosecution Service. Her supervisor, Sgt CRAW, wishes to test her understanding around the method of instituting criminal proceedings in line with the Criminal Justice Act 2003, which details where a public prosecutor may issue a written charge which charges the person with an offence. Sgt CRAW tells PC JOSEY that at the same time as issuing a written charge, the public prosecutor must also issue a requisition or a single justice procedure notice. He then asks PC JOSEY what should happen when a written charge and requisition are issued.

Which of the following would be the correct response from PC JOSEY?

A The written charge must be served on the person concerned and the court.

B The written charge and requisition must be served on the person concerned and a copy of both must be served on the court.

C The written charge and requisition must be served on the person concerned and the written charge on the court.

D The written charge and requisition must be served on the person concerned and the requisition on the court.

Question 1.2

The Rose Garden Corporation has a principal office located in Brighton as well as several corporation outlets located in Sussex and Kent. The corporation has committed an offence under s. 1248(5) of the Companies Act 2006 (a summary only offence of a company failing to retain a person to carry out second audit or review accounts when directed to do so by Secretary of State). As a result, the corporation is summonsed in relation to the offence.

In relation to the service of such a summons (under r. 99 of the Magistrates' Courts Rules 1981), which of the comments below is correct?

A It can be served at any address associated with the corporation (the principal office or one of the outlets in Sussex or Kent).

B Such a summons cannot be served on a 'person' and must be served at the principal office in Brighton.

C It can be served at the principal office in Brighton or in person by handing it to a person holding a senior position in the corporation.

D If the summons is served personally rather than at any corporation address, it must be served on the legal representative of the corporation.

Question 1.3

DICA had been summonsed to attend court following a prosecution being taken out against him in relation to an offence that he is suspected to have committed. He has failed to appear and the court is considering whether to issue a warrant to arrest DICA.

In relation to this, which of the following is correct?

A The warrant can be issued provided the offence is an indictable offence and is punishable with imprisonment of five years or more.

B The warrant can be issued provided the offence is an indictable offence or is punishable with imprisonment and DICA has attained the age of 18.

C The warrant can be issued provided the offence is an indictable offence or is punishable with imprisonment and DICA has attained the age of 17.

D In these circumstances, a warrant for arrest cannot be issued as DICA is only suspected to have committed the offence in question.

Question 1.4

HEGGART is a witness for a trial regarding an offence of blackmail. HEGGART has failed to attend court as a witness on the date and time specified. Under certain circumstances, a warrant can be issued to arrest a witness and compel them to attend court. The power for this comes from the Magistrates' Courts Act 1980.

In which of the following circumstances can a warrant be issued?

A Where a witness is appearing at magistrates' court only, and only where they have failed to comply with a witness summons.

B Where a witness is appearing at Crown Court only, and only where they have failed to comply with a witness summons.

C Where a witness is appearing at Crown Court only, and only where the judge is certain that it is in the interests of justice to compel the witness to attend.

D In any court where it is in the interests of justice to secure the attendance of a witness and where there is evidence that a summons would not ensure attendance.

Question 1.5

WATKINS is a civilian enforcement officer who is executing a warrant of arrest. The male who is the subject of the warrant demands that WATKINS gives him his name.

Which of the following is correct regarding the information WATKINS is required to show in relation to executing the warrant?

A WATKINS must provide documentary evidence of his name.

B WATKINS must provide his name, but this can be done verbally.

C WATKINS need only give documentary evidence showing the authority by which he is employed.

D WATKINS need only give documentary evidence showing that he is authorised to execute warrants.

Question 1.6

Constable McCOLL is a police officer working for the Police Service of Scotland (Police Scotland) and is on holiday in London. As he is walking along a street in London, he sees HUGHES, a male from Dundee, Scotland, whom he knows has been charged with rape and knows that a warrant has been issued by the courts in Dundee for his arrest.

Can Constable McCOLL arrest HUGHES under the warrant?

A Yes, a warrant for the arrest of a person issued in Scotland may be executed in England and Wales.

B Yes, but only if Constable McCOLL is accompanied by a police officer working for the force in which the arrest takes place.

C No, a warrant issued in Scotland cannot be executed outside Scotland.

D No, however a local officer could make the arrest properly executing the warrant.

Question 1.7

McGWYER is a civilian enforcement officer employed by the local court and author-ised in the prescribed manner. McGWYER is executing a distress warrant at an ad-dress when he notices RYAN, for whom he knows an arrest warrant has been issued, walking past the address where the distress warrant is being executed. McGWYER does not have this warrant in his possession.

Can McGWYER execute the warrant for arrest?

A Yes, a civilian enforcement officer can execute any warrant.

B Yes, an arrest warrant can be executed by a civilian enforcement officer.

C No, a civilian enforcement officer must have possession of an arrest warrant.

D No, a civilian enforcement officer cannot execute an arrest warrant.

Question 1.8

Constable GRAVES, from South Wales Police, carried out a check on the Police National Computer (PNC) on a male. The check showed that a warrant was outstanding against the male and that it had been issued in the Isle of Man.

Which of the following is correct in relation to the officer executing the warrant?

A The warrant can be executed provided the offence to which it relates corres-ponds to an offence in England and Wales.

B The warrant can be executed as all warrants issued in the Isle of Man can be exe-cuted in England and Wales.

C Warrants from the Isle of Man may be executed in England and Wales where they have been endorsed by a justice of the peace.

D Warrants from the Isle of Man may be executed in England and Wales where they have been endorsed by a district judge.

Question 1.9

DC MATHERS is dealing with a case at magistrates' court where a material witness has refused to attend. The officer also believes that they will not respond to a sum-mons and is considering applying for the district judge to issue a warrant to arrest the witness.

In relation to this, which of the following is correct?

A The officer must satisfy the district judge that it is in the interests of justice to secure the attendance of a person who could give material evidence.

B The officer must satisfy the district judge that it is in the interests of justice to secure the attendance of a person who could give material evidence, and that a summons would not procure the attendance of the person.

C The officer must satisfy the district judge by giving evidence on oath that it is in the interests of justice to secure the attendance of a person who could give material evidence.

D The officer must satisfy the district judge by giving evidence on oath that it is in the interests of justice to secure the attendance of a person who could give material evidence, and that a summons would not procure the attendance of the person.

Question 1.10

Constable DEAKINS has been trying to execute an arrest warrant issued by the court; however, the officer cannot trace the individual's correct address. The officer believes that HMRC has details of the individual and the court wishes to make a disclosure order under s. 125CA of the Magistrates' Courts Act 1980.

In these circumstances, which of the following is correct?

A HMRC are not a relevant public authority within this section and are not subject to a disclosure order.

B The court can ask HMRC to provide his name, address, date of birth or national insurance number.

C The court can ask HMRC to provide his name and address only.

D The court can ask HMRC to provide his name, address and date of birth only.

ANSWERS

Answer 1.1

Answer **B** — Section 29(3) of the Criminal Justice Act 2003 states:

> Where a relevant prosecutor issues a written charge and a requisition, the written charge and requisition must be served on the person concerned, and a copy of both must be served on the court named in the requisition.

So answers A, C and D are therefore incorrect.

Evidence and Procedure, para. 2.1.2

Answer 1.2

Answer **C** — Rule 99 of the Magistrates' Courts Rules 1981, as amended by the Magistrates' Courts (Amendment) Rules 2019 (SI 2019/1367), states:

(1) Subject to paragraph (7), a summons requiring a person to appear before a magistrates' court may be served by—
   (a) handing it to the person in person or, where the person is a corporation, to a person holding a senior position in that corporation;
   (b) posting it to the person at an address where it is reasonably believed that the person will receive it or, where the person is a corporation, the address for service in accordance with paragraph (2);

Paragraph 2 states that where the person is a corporation, the address for service under this rule is the person's principal office, and if there is no readily identifiable principal office, then any place where it carries on its activities or business.

Answer A is incorrect as the corporation has a principal office and if the summons was served at an address then that is the place it should be served rather than at one of the outlets in Sussex or Kent. Answer B is incorrect as the summons can be served personally (r. 99(1)(a))—the same section makes answer D incorrect (it does not have to be served on the legal representative of the company when being served personally).

Evidence and Procedure, para. 2.1.3

Answer 1.3

Answer **B** — An arrest warrant can be issued for a suspect by a justice of the peace if an information in writing is laid before them that a person has committed *or is suspected of having committed an offence* (s. 1(1)(b) and (3) of the Magistrates' Courts Act 1980), making answer D incorrect. Such warrants can only be issued for persons aged 18 or over (answer C is therefore incorrect) if the offence the warrant relates to is an indictable offence or is punishable with imprisonment—there is no limit to this, answer A is therefore incorrect—*or* the person's address is not sufficiently established for a summons or written charge and requisition to be served on him/her (s. 1(4)).

It is clear that a summons was not sufficiently served as the defendant has failed to comply with it, the fact it was served alone is not enough; answer D is therefore incorrect.

Evidence and Procedure, para. 2.1.5.1

Answer 1.4

Answer **D** — The Magistrates' Courts Act 1980 provides that a justice of the peace may issue a warrant where he/she is satisfied that it is in the interests of justice to secure the attendance of a person who could give material evidence. However, a warrant may only be issued where the justice of the peace is satisfied, by evidence on oath, that a summons would not procure the attendance of the person (s. 97(2)). In addition, a warrant may also be issued where a person fails to attend the court in answer to a summons where there is proof of its service if it appears to the court that there is no just excuse for the failure (s. 97(3)).

Answers A, B and C are therefore incorrect.

Evidence and Procedure, para. 2.1.5.1

Answer 1.5

Answer **A** — Rule 13.5 of the Criminal Procedure Rules 2020 states:

(1) A warrant may be executed—
    (a) by any person to whom it is directed; or
    (b) if the warrant was issued by a magistrates' court, by anyone authorised to do so by section 125(b) (warrants), 125A (civilian enforcement officers) or 125B(d) (execution by approved enforcement agency) of the Magistrates' Courts Act 1980.
(2) The person who executes a warrant must—
    (a) explain, in terms the defendant can understand, what the warrant requires, and why;

(b) show the defendant the warrant, if that person has it; and

(c) if the defendant asks—

    (i) arrange for the defendant to see the warrant, if that person does not have it, and

    (ii) show the defendant any written statement of that person's authority required by section 125A or 125B of the 1980 Act.

All of this must be shown by WATKINS, not just the authority by which he is employed and the fact he is authorised to execute warrants; answers C and D are therefore incorrect. The proof must be documentary and not just provided orally; answer B is therefore incorrect.

Evidence and Procedure, para. 2.1.6

Answer 1.6

Answer **A** — The warrant can be executed by Constable McCOLL as s. 136(2) of the Criminal Justice and Public Order Act 1994 states:

A warrant issued in—

(a) Scotland; or

(b) Northern Ireland,

for the arrest of a person charged with an offence may (without any endorsement) be executed in England and Wales by any constable of any police force of the country of issue or of the country of execution, or by a constable appointed under section 24 of the Railways and Transport Safety Act 2003, as well as by any other persons within the directions of the warrant.

Making answers C and D incorrect. The officer is from the country of origin and can make the arrest (correct answer A). There is no requirement for the arresting officer to be accompanied by a police officer working in the force area in which the arrest is being made, making answer B incorrect.

Evidence and Procedure, para. 2.1.6.2

Answer 1.7

Answer **B** — Section 125 of the Magistrates' Courts Act 1980 provides that a warrant issued by a magistrates' court may be executed by any person to whom it is directed or by any constable acting within that constable's police area.

Certain warrants issued by a magistrates' court (arrest, commitment, detention, distress or in connection with the enforcement of a fine or other order) may be executed anywhere in England and Wales by a civilian enforcement officer (s. 125A), or by an approved enforcement agency (s. 125B); answer D is therefore incorrect. However, this does not extend to all warrants; answer A is therefore incorrect. An arrest warrant is one of those that can be executed by a civilian enforcement officer, but it does not stipulate that the warrant has to be in the officer's possession; answer C is therefore incorrect.

Evidence and Procedure, para. 2.1.6

Answer 1.8

Answer **C** — Section 13 of the Indictable Offences Act 1848 provides that warrants from the Isle of Man and the Channel Islands may be executed in England and Wales where they have been endorsed by a justice of the peace; answers A, B and D are therefore incorrect.

Evidence and Procedure, para. 2.1.6.2

Answer 1.9

Answer **D** — The Magistrates' Courts Act 1980 provides that a justice of the peace may issue a warrant where they are satisfied that it is in the interests of justice to secure the attendance of a person who could give material evidence. However, a warrant may only be issued where the justice of the peace is satisfied, by evidence on oath, that a summons would not procure the attendance of the person (s. 97(2)). In addition, a warrant may also be issued where a person fails to attend the court in answer to a summons where there is proof of its service, if it appears to the court that there is no just excuse for the failure (s. 97(3)).

The person issuing the warrant must be satisfied of both parts, and the evidence must be on oath; answers A, B and C are therefore incorrect.

Evidence and Procedure, para. 2.1.5.1

Answer 1.10

Answer **B** — Section 125CA of the Magistrates' Courts Act 1980 states:

(1) A magistrates' court may make a disclosure order if satisfied that it is necessary to do so for the purpose of executing a warrant to which this section applies.

(2) This section applies to a warrant of arrest, commitment, detention or control issued by a justice of the peace in connection with the enforcement of a fine or other order imposed or made on conviction.

(3) A disclosure order is an order requiring the person to whom it is directed to supply the designated officer for the court with any of the following information about the person to whom the warrant relates—
  (a) his name, date of birth or national insurance number;
  (b) his address (or any of his addresses).

(4) A disclosure order may be made only on the application of a person entitled to execute the warrant.

As options C and D limit the amount of information HMRC can be asked to supply (by use of the term 'only'), they are incorrect.

The disclosure order may require that basic personal information (name, date of birth, national insurance number and address or addresses) held by a relevant public authority be supplied by that authority to the court for the purpose of facilitating the enforcement of a s. 125A(1) warrant which is so specified (s. 125C(1)).

A 'relevant public authority' means a Minister of the Crown, government department, local authority or chief officer of police specified in an order made by the Lord Chancellor (s. 125C(2)). HMRC would be included in this; answer A is therefore incorrect.

Evidence and Procedure, para. 2.1.6.1

2 | Release of Person Arrested

QUESTIONS

Question 2.1

There are seven defendants in custody for a complicated fraud inquiry with the Financial Conduct Authority. They have all been interviewed by officers and the senior investigating officer wishes to release the defendants on police bail pending further extensive inquiries. It is anticipated that some of the defendants may be on bail for several months.

In relation to this, which of the following is correct?

A There is no time limit for which pre-charge police bail may be granted under the Police and Criminal Evidence Act 1984.

B Although there is no time limit for which pre-charge police bail may be granted under the Police and Criminal Evidence Act 1984, the courts can intervene in exceptional circumstances.

C There is a time limit of three months in which pre-charge police bail may be granted under the Police and Criminal Evidence Act 1984.

D There is a time limit of six months in which pre-charge police bail may be granted under the Police and Criminal Evidence Act 1984.

Question 2.2

The custody officer is considering whether DENNY (an adult), having been charged with an offence of burglary, should be granted bail. The investigating officer believes that bail should be refused, as she suspects that DENNY will commit further offences. The investigating officer believes this because DENNY has previously offended while on bail.

Is the previous offending on bail relevant to the custody officer's decision?

A No, any reasonable grounds for refusing bail cannot be gained from previous incidents.

B No, 'commission of further offences' relates to non-imprisonable offences only.

C Yes, provided those offences committed on bail were burglary offences.

D Yes, provided it is considered with other factors, e.g. the strength of the evidence.

Question 2.3

REED is on 'street bail' with conditions attached to the bail. He has made an application to the police to have those conditions varied, but one day later he has not heard whether the conditions have been varied.

What options, if any, are open to REED now?

A REED may apply to a magistrates' court to have the conditions varied as the police have not answered him within 24 hours of the request.

B REED may apply to a magistrates' court to have the conditions varied as the police did not respond to his request immediately.

C REED has no options; as the conditions were imposed by the police only they can vary the conditions.

D REED has no options at the moment as he will have to wait for 48 hours to elapse before he can apply to the magistrates' court for the conditions to be varied.

Question 2.4

GREENING is being bailed by the custody officer and indicates he has had enough of the local police and may well be moving away from the area to live with his brother, who is well known to police in that area. The custody officer asks for that address and if the move is imminent. GREENING replies that it's none of her business.

What is the most appropriate action that the custody officer can now take?

A The custody officer should now refuse bail as she does not know GREENING's address.

B The custody officer can impose a condition of bail that any change of address must be notified.

C The custody officer can take no action as GREENING has not indicated he is definitely moving address.

D The custody officer can take no action as the brother's address can be easily ascertained.

Question 2.5

FINCH is on police bail for a robbery offence and is due to return next week. Despite a very thorough investigation, no eye-witness has been obtained. The investigating officer asks the custody officer to supply to the defendant a notice under s. 47(4) of the Police and Criminal Evidence Act 1984 that their attendance is no longer required. This is done; however, two days later an eye-witness comes forward identifying FINCH as the robber.

Which of the following is correct in relation to action the police may now take?

A The police must serve a notice on FINCH that the bail date has been reinstated.

B The police must attend at his home address and give him a street bail notification.

C The police can re-arrest FINCH and can do so without warrant.

D The police can re-arrest FINCH, but this must be done with a warrant issued by the court.

Question 2.6

RYTON (a 13-year-old boy) committed a burglary and stole a car to make good his escape. He was spotted by the police and a short police pursuit ensued (they were unaware that the driver was a juvenile). RYTON crashed the car into parked cars and ran off; he was captured nearby by the police. RYTON is a prolific offender with many previous convictions. He has been charged with burglary and aggravated vehicle-taking. The custody officer is aware that there is no secure local authority accommodation available in the local area.

In relation to detaining RYTON at the police station, which of the following is true?

A RYTON can be detained as the police are aware that no secure local authority accommodation is available in the local area.

B RYTON can be detained as the police are aware that no secure local authority accommodation is available in the local area and there is a risk to the public by placing him in insecure accommodation.

C RYTON can be detained provided the custody officer certifies that it would have been impractical to find local authority accommodation.

D RYTON can be detained provided the custody officer investigates whether there is secure local authority accommodation available even where there is no such accommodation.

Question 2.7

DALE is making a 'live link' bail application at the police station and has attended with his solicitor to make the application to the magistrates' court. The police wish to search DALE as they want to ensure that staff at the station are kept safe.

In relation to this, which of the following is correct?

A The police have power to search DALE in these circumstances but there is no power of arrest if he refuses; the live link, however, could be cancelled.

B The police have power to search DALE in these circumstances and there is a power of arrest if he refuses.

C The police have no power to search DALE; however, if he refuses to submit to a voluntary search the live link could be cancelled.

D The police have no power to search DALE and as this is a live link bail application they have to facilitate it even if a voluntary search is refused.

Question 2.8

ROWLANDS was on unconditional bail on a charge of assault. The magistrates' court granted bail for a period of four weeks. ROWLANDS failed to appear and a warrant was issued. He was arrested three weeks later and taken before the court. When he gave evidence relating to a charge of absconding, ROWLANDS stated he had been in hospital at the time of the court date and left hospital a week later. He also stated that he had not been given a copy of the court record of the date of his next appearance.

In relation to ROWLANDS's potential offence of absconding, which of the following is true?

A ROWLANDS did not commit the offence as he had reasonable cause not to surrender.

B ROWLANDS did not commit the offence because he did not receive a copy of the court record.

C ROWLANDS still committed the offence even though he had reasonable cause.

D ROWLANDS committed the offence simply by failing to appear in the first place.

Question 2.9

WEBSTER was on bail to attend at magistrates' court at a date in the future. Constable NEWELL received firm evidence that WEBSTER was not going to surrender but was certain to abscond. Constable NEWELL arrested WEBSTER at 11.20 am on

Monday, under s. 7(3) of the Bail Act 1976, and detention was authorised at 11.50 am. WEBSTER was taken to court at 10 am on Tuesday and appeared before a justice of the peace at 12 noon. The justice is of the opinion that WEBSTER will fail to surrender in the future.

In relation to what the justice may do next, which of the following is true?

A   He may remand WEBSTER in custody as he was brought to court within 24 hours of detention being authorised.

B   He may remand WEBSTER in custody as he was brought to court within 24 hours of the time he was arrested.

C   He may not remand WEBSTER in custody as he was not put before a justice within 24 hours of detention being authorised.

D   He may not remand WEBSTER in custody as he was not put before a justice within 24 hours of the time he was arrested.

Question 2.10

BARD has been arrested on suspicion of her involvement in a number of serious offences including robbery, burglary and aggravated burglary. She denied all offences in interview but the Crown Prosecution Service has agreed to authorise charges for these serious offences. The custody officer is considering imposing a surety on BARD as part of granting her conditional bail.

In relation to this surety, which of the following is correct?

A   The surety can be imposed to ensure she surrenders to custody only.

B   The surety can be imposed to ensure she surrenders to custody only and can be stood by BARD.

C   The surety can be imposed to ensure no further offending and surrender to custody.

D   The surety can be imposed to ensure no further offending and surrender to custody; it can be stood by BARD.

Question 2.11

DEWTRY has been given street bail to attend at his local police station (which is not designated) to be interviewed in relation to a common assault.

Which of the following is true?

A   DEWTRY should not have been street bailed to a non-designated police station.

B   DEWTRY must be released within six hours of his arrival at the police station.

C DEWTRY must be released or taken to a designated police station within six hours of his arrival at the police station.

D DEWTRY must be released or taken to a designated police station within six hours of his first contact with a police officer at the police station.

Question 2.12

Constable GREIG granted street bail to HENTY and set conditions of bail. HENTY believes that these conditions are unreasonable and wishes to have them varied. He is due at Central Police Station (a designated station) on bail next week.

In relation to varying bail conditions in these circumstances, which of the following is correct?

A HENTY has to attend court to have 'street bail' conditions overturned, they cannot be varied.

B HENTY should attend at Central Police Station and request the custody officer to vary the conditions.

C HENTY should attend at Central Police Station and ask the officer in the case to vary the conditions.

D HENTY should attend at any police station and ask any officer, other than the officer in the case, to vary the conditions.

Question 2.13

KEEN stood surety for her son at court when he appeared charged with a serious fraud offence. The value of the surety is £100,000. KEEN, however, is concerned her son may not attend at court and wishes to be relieved of her obligation as surety and telephones the officer in the case to ask for that.

In relation to this, which of the following is correct?

A KEEN can only be relieved of her duties as surety by a court and needs to apply to the magistrates' court.

B KEEN can only be relieved of her duties as surety by a court and needs to apply to the court her son is next due to appear at, be that magistrates' court or Crown Court.

C KEEN will be relieved of her duties as surety following the phone call but no power of arrest exists until the notification is received in writing.

D KEEN will only be relieved of her duties as surety when she has notified the officer in writing that the accused is unlikely to surrender to custody.

Question 2.14

GREAVES has been arrested on suspicion of assaulting his partner and has been taken to the police station. Following a no comment interview, the police wish to release GREAVES for further investigations to take place.

In relation to granting pre-charge bail, which of the following is correct?
A GREAVES can be released on bail providing this is court-sanctioned.
B GREAVES can be released on bail if a set of risk factors has been considered.
C GREAVES can be released on bail but it must be conditional.
D GREAVES can be released on bail but it must be unconditional.

Question 2.15

HOEY has been arrested for an offence of rape and a decision is being considered about releasing him on bail whilst further inquiries are being conducted. The custody officer is considering 'pre-conditions for bail' and whether they should release HOEY with or without bail.

In relation to this, which of the following is correct?
A The presumption is to release without bail and therefore HOEY should be released without bail.
B The decision to release on bail if it is necessary and proportionate in all the circumstances can only ever be made by an officer of the rank of inspector or above.
C The custody officer can make the decision to release on bail if it is necessary and proportionate but this must be authorised by an officer of the rank of inspector or above.
D The custody officer can make the decision to release on bail if it is necessary and proportionate in all the circumstances, having considered any representations by HOEY or his legal representative.

Question 2.16

Officers from the Serious Fraud Office (SFO) have been investigating an organised crime group responsible for large-scale money laundering. There is an extensive amount of paperwork to be examined and the suspects are to be correctly released on bail.

From the start of the suspects' bail date, for how long can the suspects be bailed?

A 28 days.

B Three months.

C Six months.

D There is no specific time limit in SFO cases.

Question 2.17

WESTON had been released on police bail following an arrest for assault. WESTON is now no longer required to attend the police station to answer bail.

Which of the following is correct in respect of the Police and Criminal Evidence Act 1984?

A The custody officer must give notice in writing to that person that his attendance at the police station is not required.

B The custody officer should give notice in writing to that person that his attendance at the police station is not required.

C The custody officer may give notice in writing to that person that his attendance at the police station is not required.

D The custody officer does not have to give notice in writing to that person that his attendance at the police station is not required.

Question 2.18

PC KIRBY arrested STOWE (aged 17 years) for an offence of theft (contrary to s. 1(1) of the Theft Act 1968). Having considered the circumstances, PC KIRBY considered that it was necessary and proportionate to release STOWE on bail without being required to attend a police station in line with s. 30A(1A) of the Police and Criminal Evidence Act 1984. PC KIRBY subsequently obtained the necessary authority from the custody officer.

In relation to such bail, can conditions be attached?

A Yes, although no requirement to reside in a bail hostel may be imposed as a condition of such bail.

B No, bail conditions can only be imposed by a custody officer when a defendant is bailed from a designated police station.

C Yes, and this would include a requirement to provide a surety or sureties for STOWE's surrender to custody.
D No, bail conditions cannot be imposed on a person who is bailed under the terms of s. 30A when they are under 18 years of age.

Question 2.19

EASTWOOD is charged with a s. 47 assault and is released on bail with the conditions that she is not to contact the victim of the offence and that she provide a surety. COOKE acts as EASTWOOD's surety. Three days after EASTWOOD's release, COOKE telephones PC SNEEDEN (the officer in the case) and informs him that EASTWOOD is unlikely to surrender to custody and, for that reason, he wishes to be relieved of his obligations as a surety.

Considering the powers under s. 7 of the Bail Act 1976, which of the following statements is correct?
A PC SNEEDEN can arrest EASTWOOD because of the information provided to him by COOKE.
B The only reason that will allow PC SNEEDEN to arrest EASTWOOD is if he has reasonable grounds to believe EASTWOOD will break any of her bail conditions.
C PC SNEEDEN will not be able to arrest EASTWOOD because the notification by COOKE was not made in writing.
D The only reason that will allow PC SNEEDEN to arrest EASTWOOD is if he has reasonable grounds for believing that EASTWOOD is not likely to surrender to custody.

Question 2.20

CLARIDGE has been arrested in respect of an offence of robbery but there are numerous inquiries to carry out in relation to the investigation. Having examined the circumstances, it is decided that bail is appropriate (the pre-conditions for bail being satisfied).

Which of the comments below is correct in relation to the granting of bail in these circumstances?
A Any representations made by CLARIDGE regarding bail should be noted but such representations are not relevant to the granting of bail.

B The 'applicable bail period' for CLARIDGE will begin on the day he was arrested for the offence of robbery.

C It is possible for CLARIDGE's bail to be extended from 28 days to six months but this extension must be authorised by an officer of inspector rank or above.

D CLARIDGE's bail could not be extended for a period longer than three months.

Question 2.21

KHATUN has been charged with an offence of attempted rape and the issue of bail is now being considered. KHATUN has a previous conviction for manslaughter, for which he served five years' imprisonment (that manslaughter conviction is 12 years old) but he has no other previous convictions.

Will the provisions of s. 25 of the Criminal Justice and Public Order Act 1994 be applicable in these circumstances?

A Yes, as KHATUN will not be granted bail unless there are exceptional circumstances which justify it.

B No, as KHATUN's previous conviction for manslaughter is over ten years old.

C Yes, due to the nature of the charge and because of KHATUN's previous conviction, he cannot be granted bail.

D No, as s. 25 only relates to defendants charged with murder, attempted murder or manslaughter.

Question 2.22

BROWN has been charged with an offence of burglary and has been bailed by PS KING (the custody officer). PS KING imposed a number of bail conditions upon BROWN, including a curfew between set times. One week after being bailed, BROWN finds out that his girlfriend is pregnant and wants to have his bail condition of curfew modified so that he can help his girlfriend during her pregnancy.

Which of the following comments is correct in respect of varying the bail condition?

A BROWN must speak to PS KING who is the only person who can vary the conditions of bail.

B BROWN's conditions of bail can be varied by PS KING or another custody officer serving at any police station in PS KING's force area.

2. Release of Person Arrested

C BROWN's conditions of bail can be varied by PS KING or another custody officer serving at the same police station that PS KING works at.
D BROWN's conditions of bail can be varied but only by a magistrates' court.

Question 2.23

Magistrates have made a 'live link bail' direction (under s. 57C of the Crime and Disorder Act 1998) in relation to CRABTREE (a male defendant) who is being prosecuted for a number of different offences. CRABTREE has been directed to attend the preliminary hearing of his case through a live link at a police station and duly attends the police station at the appointed time. PCs SAMUEL (a male police officer) and ORWELL (a female designated detention officer) are directed to deal with CRABTREE and want to know the extent of their powers to search CRABTREE under s. 54B of the Police and Criminal Evidence Act 1984.

Which of the following statements is true with regard to the power under s. 54B?
A Either officer may search CRABTREE although seizure of items found as a consequence of the search can only take place if the searching officer reasonably believes the thing to be seized is evidence of an offence.
B The power of search under s. 54B is available to PC SAMUEL only as he is a male police officer; it is not available to designated detention officers.
C Any police officer or designated detention officer may use the search power. The sex of the police officer or designated detention officer is irrelevant.
D Only PC SAMUEL may search CRABTREE; the officer may also search any article CRABTREE has in his possession. If CRABTREE refuses to be searched, he can be arrested.

Question 2.24

BARKER and MORTON are arrested and charged with an offence of burglary. They are both bailed by the police to appear at a magistrates' court. On the day they are due to appear at the magistrates' court, BARKER's car will not start, meaning that he arrives in the court building 30 minutes late for his court appearance. As he has missed his breakfast, he visits a cafe in the court building to have something to eat—when he finally turns up for his court appearance, he is actually 60 minutes late. MORTON does not appear at all as he has made a genuine mistake about the day he was supposed to appear and thinks his court appearance is set for the following day.

Which of the statements below is correct in relation to liability for an offence of absconding (under s. 6 of the Bail Act 1976)?

A BARKER would be able to say that he has a 'reasonable cause' for failing to surrender to custody and does not commit the offence.

B Being mistaken about the day on which one should have appeared in court has been held to be a 'reasonable excuse' for failing to answer bail so MORTON would not commit this offence.

C BARKER and MORTON both commit the offence in these circumstances.

D The offence has not been committed as the offence of absconding under s. 6 only relates to failing to surrender to custody when bail has been granted by a court rather than the police.

ANSWERS

Answer 2.1

Answer **D** — When the custody officer is releasing a person on bail to attend at a police station under s. 47(3)(c) of the Police and Criminal Evidence Act 1984, he/she must appoint a time on the day on which the 'applicable bail period' in relation to the person ends (s. 47ZA(1) and (2)). The 'applicable bail period', in relation to a person, means in a Financial Conduct Authority case, HMRC case, National Crime Agency case or Serious Fraud Office case the period of six months beginning with the person's bail start date (s. 47ZB(1)(a)) and in any other case the period of three months beginning with the person's bail start date (s. 47ZB(1)(b)). Therefore answers A, B and C are incorrect.

Evidence and Procedure, para. 2.2.3.2

Answer 2.2

Answer **D** — The Police and Criminal Evidence Act 1984, s. 38(1) provides that where an arrested person is charged with an offence, the custody officer, subject to s. 25 of the Criminal Justice and Public Order Act 1994, need not grant bail if the person arrested *is not an arrested juvenile* and one or more of the following grounds apply:

  (a) the person's name or address cannot be ascertained or the custody officer has reasonable grounds for doubting whether a name or address furnished is that person's real name or address;
  (b) the custody officer has reasonable grounds for believing that the person arrested will fail to appear in court to answer to bail;
  (c) in the case of a person arrested for an imprisonable offence, the custody officer has reasonable grounds for believing that the detention of the person arrested is necessary to prevent him/her from committing an offence;
  (d) in a case of a person aged 18 or over, where a sample may be taken from the person under s. 63B (where there is a provision for drug testing in force for that police area and station), the custody officer has reasonable grounds for believing that the detention of the person is necessary to enable the sample to be taken;
  (e) in the case of a person arrested for an offence which is not an imprisonable offence, the custody officer has reasonable grounds for believing that the detention of the person arrested is necessary to prevent him/her from causing physical injury to any other person or from causing loss of or damage to property;

(f) the custody officer has reasonable grounds for believing that the detention of the person arrested is necessary to prevent him/her from interfering with the administration of justice or with the investigation of offences or of a particular offence;

(g) the custody officer has reasonable grounds for believing that the detention of the person arrested is necessary for his/her own protection; or

(h) the person is charged with murder.

If the person arrested is *an arrested juvenile* and one or more of the following grounds apply:

- any of the requirements of paras (a) to (h) above but, in the case of para. (d), only if the arrested juvenile has attained the minimum age;
- the custody officer has reasonable grounds for believing that the arrested juvenile ought to be detained in his/her own interests.

Although there are grounds for refusing bail that relate to non-imprisonable offences only, the one relating to 'commission of further offences' relates to imprisonable offences only (i.e. burglary), and therefore answer B is incorrect. The previous offending is not specific to the offence currently charged and would therefore relate to any offence, and therefore answer C is incorrect—it is information which should be taken as a factor by the custody officer.

The defendant need not be granted bail if the court (custody officer) is satisfied that there are substantial grounds for believing that the defendant, if released on bail (whether subject to conditions or not) would:

- fail to surrender to custody, or
- commit an offence while on bail …

The custody officer will have regard to considerations as appear to be relevant in making his/her decision and they include the defendant's record as respects the fulfilment of his/her obligations under previous grants of bail in criminal proceedings; answer A is therefore incorrect.

Evidence and Procedure, para. 2.2.6

Answer 2.3

Answer **D** — Section 30CB(1) of the Police and Criminal Evidence Act 1984 states:

Where a person released on bail under s. 30A(1) is on bail subject to conditions, a magistrates' court may, on an application by or on behalf of the person, vary the conditions if:

(a) the conditions have been varied under s. 30CA(1) since being imposed under s. 30A(3B),

(b) a request for variation under s. 30CA(1) of the conditions has been made and re-fused, or

(c) a request for variation under s. 30CA(1) of the conditions has been made and the period of 48 hours beginning with the day when the request was made has expired without the request having been withdrawn or the conditions having been varied in response to the request.

REED will have to wait until the end of the 48-hour period prior to applying to the magistrates' court to have his conditions varied depending on him not withdrawing the request or the police varying the conditions within that time period. Answers A, B and C are therefore incorrect.

Evidence and Procedure, para. 2.2.2.5

Answer 2.4

Answer **B** — Under s. 3A of the Bail Act 1976, conditions can be imposed where it is necessary to do so for the purpose of preventing a person from:

• failing to surrender to custody; or
• committing an offence while on bail; or
• interfering with witnesses or otherwise obstructing the course of justice, whether in relation to him/herself or any other person.

One or more of the following conditions can be imposed:

• the accused is to live and sleep at a specified address;
• the accused is to notify any changes of address;
• the accused is to report periodically (daily, weekly or at other intervals) to their local police station;
• the accused is restricted from entering a certain area or building or to go within a specified distance of a specified address;
• the accused is not to contact (whether directly or indirectly) the victim of the al-leged offence and/or any other probable prosecution witness;
• the accused is to surrender his/her passport and/or identity card;
• the accused's movements are restricted by an imposed curfew between set times (i.e. when it is thought the accused might commit offences or come into contact with witnesses);
• the accused is required to provide a surety or security.

It is incorrect to state that there is no action the custody officer can take. Where he/she feels that it is necessary to ensure surrender to custody, he/she may impose a condition of bail that any change of address must be notified; answers C and D are therefore incorrect. The grounds for refusing bail are that the person's name and address cannot be ascertained or that which is given is doubted. This is not the case here as the police know who GREENING is and have an address, they even have an indication where GREENING intends to go (although no actual definitive intent was given). The brother is known therefore his address can be ascertained; it would not be the most appropriate action to deny bail in these circumstances; answer A is therefore incorrect.

Evidence and Procedure, para. 2.2.7.2

Answer 2.5

Answer **C** — The Police and Criminal Evidence Act 1984 provides that a person may be released on bail with a duty to surrender at a given time and date while inquiries are ongoing.

A custody officer, having granted bail to a person subject to a duty to appear at a police station, may give notice in writing to that person that his/her attendance at the police station is not required (s. 47(4A) and (4B)).

However, nothing in the Bail Act prevents the re-arrest without warrant (answer D is therefore incorrect) of a person released on bail subject to a duty to attend at a police station if new evidence justifying a further arrest has come to light since their release (s. 47(2)).

Answers A and B both include 'must do' but, as stated, there is nothing preventing re-arrest; they are both incorrect.

Evidence and Procedure, para. 2.2.3

Answer 2.6

Answer **D** — The Children (Secure Accommodation) Regulations 1991 (SI 1991/1505 as amended by SI 2012/3134 and SI 2015/1883) provide that a child who is detained by the police under s. 38(6) of the Police and Criminal Evidence Act 1984, and who is aged 12 or over but under the age of 17, must be moved to local authority accommodation unless the custody officer certifies that it is impracticable for him/her to do so, or that no secure accommodation is available and local authority accommodation would be inadequate to protect the child or public from serious harm. Where no secure accommodation is available and the serious harm criterion is met, the child can be kept in police detention. But it is not enough to just use knowledge that there is no secure accommodation to fulfil the responsibility to find such accommodation. In *R (On the Application of BG) v Chief Constable of the West Midlands Constabulary* [2014] EWHC 4374 (Admin), it was held that the police were fulfilling their responsibilities by investigating whether secure local authority accommodation was available even where there was no such accommodation available. In every case, the police must make inquiries about secure accommodation before authorising police detention; answers A, B and C are therefore incorrect.

Evidence and Procedure, para. 2.2.6

Answer 2.7

Answer **B** — The Police and Criminal Evidence Act 1984, s. 54B states:

(1) A constable may search at any time—
   (a) any person who is at a police station to answer to live link bail; and
   (b) any article in the possession of such a person.
(2) If the constable reasonably believes a thing in the possession of the person ought to be seized on any of the grounds mentioned in subsection (3), the constable may seize and retain it or cause it to be seized and retained.
(3) The grounds are that the thing—
   (a) may jeopardise the maintenance of order in the police station;
   (b) may put the safety of any person in the police station at risk; or
   (c) may be evidence of, or in relation to, an offence ...

Answers C and D are therefore incorrect.

Section 46A(1ZB) (see *Evidence and Procedure*, para. 2.2.3.3) provides a constable with a power of arrest for defendants who attend the police station to answer live link bail but refuse to be searched under s. 54B; answer A is therefore incorrect.

Evidence and Procedure, paras 2.2.3.3, 2.2.4.1

Answer 2.8

Answer **C** — Section 6 of the Bail Act 1976 creates the offence of absconding. By s. 6(1), if a person released on bail fails without reasonable cause to surrender to custody, he/she is guilty of an offence. The burden of showing reasonable cause is on the accused (s. 6(3)). Moreover, a person who had reasonable cause for failing to surrender on the appointed day nevertheless commits an offence if he/she fails to surrender *as soon after the appointed time as is reasonably practicable* (s. 6(2)). The fact that ROWLANDS did not surrender to the court until being arrested means that, although he had reasonable cause, he failed to surrender and therefore still commits the offence (answer A is therefore incorrect). The offence is not absolute and is not committed simply by failing to surrender to custody, and therefore answer D is incorrect.

Section 6(4) of the 1976 Act states:

> A failure to give a person granted bail in criminal proceedings a copy of the record of the decision shall not constitute a reasonable cause for that person's failure to surrender to custody.

Therefore answer B is incorrect.

Evidence and Procedure, para. 2.2.9

Answer 2.9

Answer **D** — Section 7(3) of the Bail Act 1976 states:

> A person who has been released on bail in criminal proceedings and is under a duty to surrender into the custody of a court may be arrested without warrant by a constable—
>
> (a) if the constable has reasonable grounds for believing that that person is not likely to surrender to custody...

Following arrest under s. 7(3), the person arrested must be brought before a magistrate as soon as practicable, and in any event within 24 hours (s. 7(4)). Note that the section clearly states that the person must be brought before a magistrate (justice) and not brought merely to the court precincts, and therefore answers A and B are incorrect. This requirement is absolute and requires that a detainee be brought not merely to the court precincts or cells but actually be dealt with by a justice within 24 hours of being arrested (*R (On the Application of Culley)* v *Crown Court sitting at Dorchester* [2007] EWHC 109 (Admin)). The 24 hours is calculated from the time of arrest and not the time detention was authorised and therefore answer C is incorrect.

Evidence and Procedure, para. 2.2.8

Answer 2.10

Answer **A** — Section 8 of the Bail Act 1976 states:

> (1) This section applies where a person is granted bail in criminal proceedings on condition that he provides one or more surety or sureties for the purpose of securing that he surrenders to custody...

This section has been tested in the courts and it has been held that there is no power to grant conditional bail with a surety to ensure no further offending; a surety can be sought only for the purpose of securing surrender to custody and not for any other purpose (*R (On the Application of Shea)* v *Winchester Crown Court* [2013] EWHC 1050 (Admin)); answers C and D are therefore incorrect.

A person cannot stand as his/her own surety (s. 3(2) of the 1976 Act); answer B is therefore incorrect.

Evidence and Procedure, para. 2.2.7.4

Answer 2.11

Answer **C** — The Criminal Justice Act 2003 allows an officer to 'street bail' an offender as an alternative to arresting him/her and taking him/her straight to the police station, as was required by s. 30 of the Police and Criminal Evidence Act 1984 prior to being amended by the 2003 Act.

Section 30C(2) states:

If a person is required to attend a police station which is not a designated police station [answer A is therefore incorrect] he must be—

(a) released, or
(b) taken to a designated police station,

not more than six hours after his arrival.

Answers B and D are therefore incorrect.

Evidence and Procedure, para. 2.2.2.3

Answer 2.12

Answer **B** — Section 30CA(1) of the Police and Criminal Evidence Act 1984 states:

Where a person released under section 30A(1) of the Police and Criminal Evidence Act is on bail subject to conditions—

(a) a relevant officer at the police station at which the person is required to attend, may, at the request of the person but subject to subsection (2), vary the conditions.

As the conditions can be varied, answer A is therefore incorrect. The 'relevant officer' in relation to a designated police station means a custody officer, but in relation to any other police station means a constable who is not involved in the investigation of the relevant offence, if readily available, and, if not available, the constable who granted bail (s. 30CA(5)); answer C is therefore incorrect. HENTY was given notice of which police station to attend, so cannot attend any police station; answer D is therefore incorrect.

Evidence and Procedure, para. 2.2.2.4

Answer 2.13

Answer **D** — Section 8 of the Bail Act 1976 states:

(1) This section applies where a person is granted bail in criminal proceedings on condition that he provides one or more surety or sureties for the purpose of securing that he surrenders to custody.
(2) In considering the suitability for that purpose of a proposed surety, regard may be had (amongst other things) to—
   (a) the surety's financial resources;
   (b) his character and any previous convictions of his; and
   (c) his proximity (whether in point of kinship, place of residence or otherwise) to the person for whom he is to be surety.

The Bail Act 1976 provides that a surety may notify a constable in writing that the accused is unlikely to surrender to custody and, for that reason, he/she wishes to be relieved of his/her obligations as surety. This written notification provides a constable with the power to arrest the accused without warrant (s. 7(3)). It is the officer who received the notification not the courts; answers A and B are therefore incorrect. It only applies when it is made in writing not a phone call; answer C is therefore incorrect.

Evidence and Procedure, para. 2.2.7.4

Answer 2.14

Answer **B** — The release of persons arrested is regulated by the Bail Act 1976, the Police and Criminal Evidence Act 1984 and the Criminal Justice and Public Order Act 1994. Significant changes to the existing legislation have been made by the Police, Crime, Sentencing and Courts Act 2022. The 2022 Act establishes a neutral position within the legislation by removing the presumption against pre-charge bail. It creates a set of risk factors to be taken into account when considering whether to grant pre-charge bail, therefore making answer B correct. The Act makes particular reference to the safeguarding of the victim, witness and/or suspect, particularly where they are vulnerable. The officer granting bail may consider attaching conditions relevant and proportionate to the suspect and the offence, therefore answers C and D are incorrect. Answer A is also incorrect as there is no requirement for this pre-charge bail to be court-based and it can be granted by the custody officer. The reference to a custody officer in s. 30A(1A)(b) includes a reference to an officer other than a custody officer who is performing the functions of a custody officer where a custody officer is not readily available (s. 36(7C)).

Evidence and Procedure, paras 2.2.1, 2.2.2.1

Answer 2.15

Answer **D** — The Police and Criminal Evidence Act 1984, s. 50A states:

For the purposes of this Part the following are the pre-conditions for bail in relation to the release of a person by a custody officer—

(a) that the custody officer is satisfied that releasing the person on bail is necessary and proportionate in all the circumstances (having regard, in particular, to any conditions of bail which would be imposed), and
(b) that the custody officer has considered any representations made by the person or the person's legal representative.

Answer A is therefore incorrect as the presumption against pre-charge bail was removed by the Police, Crime, Sentencing and Courts Act 2022. Answers B and C are incorrect as, again, this legislation removed the authority for such bail laying with an officer of the rank of inspector or above. Therefore the correct answer is D.

Evidence and Procedure, para. 2.2.3.1

Answer 2.16

Answer **C** — When the custody officer is releasing a person on bail to attend at a police station under s. 47(3)(c), he/she must appoint a time on the day on which the 'applicable bail period' in relation to the person ends (s. 47ZA(1) and (2)). The 'applicable bail period', in relation to a person, means in a Financial Conduct Authority case, HMRC case, National Crime Agency case or Serious Fraud Office case the period of six months beginning with the person's bail start date (s. 47ZB(1)(a)) and, in any other case, the period of three months beginning with the person's bail start date (s. 47ZB(1)(b)). Answers A, B and D are therefore incorrect.

Evidence and Procedure, para. 2.2.3.2

Answer 2.17

Answer **C** — Section 47(4) of the Police and Criminal Evidence Act 1984 states that where a custody officer has granted bail to a person subject to a duty to appear at a police station, the custody officer *may* give notice in writing to that person that his attendance at the police station is not required. Therefore answers A, B and D are incorrect.

Evidence and Procedure, para. 2.2.4

Answer 2.18

Answer **A** — The Police and Criminal Evidence Act 1984, s. 30A provides for persons arrested elsewhere than at a police station to be released with or without bail without being required to attend a police station. Answer B is incorrect as conditions may be imposed (s. 30A(3B)). The age of the person concerned does not have a bearing on the ability to impose conditions, making answer D incorrect. Whilst conditions may be imposed, there are limitations and s. 30A(3A)(c) states that where a constable releases a person on such bail the person shall not be required to provide a surety or sureties for his/her surrender to custody, making answer C incorrect. Section 30A(3A)(d) states that no requirement to reside in a bail hostel may be imposed as a condition of bail (correct answer A).

Evidence and Procedure, para. 2.2.2.1

Answer 2.19

Answer **C** — Section 7 of the Bail Act 1976 provides three occasions when a constable may arrest a person released on bail: (a) if the constable has reasonable grounds for believing that the person is not likely to surrender to custody; (b) if the constable has reasonable grounds for believing that the person is likely to break any of the conditions of their bail or has reasonable grounds for suspecting that the person has broken any of those conditions; or (c) in a case where that person was released on bail with one or more surety or sureties, if a surety notifies a constable in writing that the person is unlikely to surrender to custody and for that reason the surety wishes to be relieved of their obligations as a surety. Answers B and D are incorrect as the Act provides three grounds for arrest and not one. Answer A is incorrect because the notification must be made in writing.

Evidence and Procedure, paras 2.2.7.4, 2.2.8

Answer 2.20

Answer **C** — The Police and Criminal Evidence Act 1984, s. 50A states:

> For the purposes of this Part the following are the pre-conditions for bail in relation to the release of a person by a custody officer—
>
> (a) that the custody officer is satisfied that releasing the person on bail is necessary and proportionate in all the circumstances (having regard, in particular, to any conditions of bail which would be imposed), and
> (b) that the custody officer has considered any representations made by the person or the person's legal representative.

Therefore answer A is incorrect. The 'applicable bail period', in relation to a person, means in a Financial Conduct Authority case, HMRC case, National Crime Agency case or Serious Fraud Office case the period of six months beginning with the person's bail start date (s. 47ZB(1)(a)) and, in any other case, the period of three months beginning with the person's bail start date (s. 47ZB(1)(b)). A person's bail start date is the day after the day on which the person was arrested for the relevant offence. Therefore answer B is incorrect. Section 47ZD allows a relevant officer (an officer of the rank of inspector or above) to extend bail from 28 days to six months where the conditions A to D set out in s. 47ZC are met. Therefore answer C is correct and answer D is incorrect.

Evidence and Procedure, paras 2.2.3.1, 2.2.3.2

Answer 2.21

Answer **A** — Section 25 of the Criminal Justice and Public Order Act 1994 applies when a defendant is charged with murder, attempted murder, manslaughter and a host of offences under the Sexual Offences Act 2003 and has a conviction for one of those offences. This makes answer D incorrect. There are no time limitations relating to when the previous conviction was obtained, making answer B incorrect. A defendant charged with one of the above offences, and with a previous conviction for one of the above offences, will not be granted bail unless there are exceptional circumstances which justify it, making answer C incorrect.

Evidence and Procedure, para. 2.2.5

Answer 2.22

Answer **C** — Section 3A(4) of the Bail Act 1976 states that where a custody officer has granted bail in criminal proceedings, he/she or *another custody officer* serving at the *same police station* may, at the request of the person to whom it was granted, vary the conditions of bail and, in doing so, he/she may impose conditions or more serious conditions, making answers A, B and D incorrect.

Evidence and Procedure, para. 2.2.7.3

Answer 2.23

Answer **D** — Section 54B of the Police and Criminal Evidence Act 1984 states:

(1) A constable may search at any time—
   (a) any person who is at a police station to answer to live link bail; and
   (b) any article in the possession of such a person.
(2) If the constable reasonably believes a thing in the possession of the person ought to be seized on any of the grounds mentioned in subsection (3), the constable may seize and retain it or cause it to be seized and retained.
(3) The grounds are that the thing—
   (a) may jeopardise the maintenance of order in the police station;
   (b) may put the safety of any person in the police station at risk; or
   (c) may be evidence of, or in relation to, an offence.
(4) The constable may record or cause to be recorded all or any of the things seized and retained pursuant to subsection (2).
(5) An intimate search may not be carried out under this section.
(6) The constable carrying out a search under subsection (1) must be of the same sex as the person being searched.

Designated detention officers, as well as constables, can use the power. So although the power is available to PC ORWELL (making answer B incorrect), she cannot search CRABTREE as the searching officer and person searched have to be of the same sex (making answer A incorrect). Answer C is incorrect as s. 54B(3) provides three reasons why property might be seized by the searching officer. Answer D is correct as PC SAMUEL is the only officer who can search CRABTREE and articles in his possession. Section 46A(1ZB) provides a constable with a power of arrest for defendants who attend the police station to answer live link bail but refuse to be searched under s. 54B.

Evidence and Procedure, para. 2.2.4.1

Answer 2.24

Answer **C** — The Bail Act 1976, s. 6 creates two offences in relation to absconding and states:

(1) If a person who has been released on bail in criminal proceedings fails without reasonable cause to surrender to custody he shall be guilty of an offence.

2. Release of Person Arrested

(2) If a person who—
   (a) has been released on bail in criminal proceedings, and
   (b) having reasonable cause therefore, has failed to surrender to custody, fails to surrender to custody at the appointed place as soon after the appointed time as is reasonably practicable he shall be guilty of an offence.

Section 6 applies where:

* the police grant bail to a suspect to appear at the police station;
* the police grant bail to a defendant to appear at court on the first appearance (making answer D incorrect);
* the court grants bail to the defendant to return to court at a later date.

A person who has 'reasonable cause' still commits the offence if he/she fails to surrender 'as soon after the appointed time as is reasonably practicable'. Where an accused was half an hour late in appearing at court, it was held that he/she had absconded (*R* v *Scott* [2007] EWCA Crim 2757). In *Laidlaw* v *Atkinson* (1986) The Times, 2 August, it was held that being mistaken about the day on which one should have appeared was not a reasonable excuse. This means that answers A and B are incorrect—both men commit the offence (correct answer C).

Evidence and Procedure, para. 2.2.9

3 | Court Procedure and Witnesses

QUESTIONS

Question 3.1

BIRD is appearing at Crown Court charged with grievous bodily harm (under s. 18 of the Offences Against the Person Act 1861). He has decided to conduct his own case and is accompanied by a friend, COOPER, as an adviser.

In relation to what COOPER can do in court, which of the following is correct?

A COOPER can advise BIRD.

B COOPER can advise BIRD and ask questions of witnesses.

C COOPER can advise BIRD and address the court.

D COOPER can advise BIRD, question witnesses and address the court.

Question 3.2

Constable GUNTER and Constable HUNT are witnesses in a case of theft. Both officers made pocket notebook entries regarding the incident, and have refreshed their memory from those notebooks prior to giving evidence. Constable GUNTER is now giving her evidence-in-chief and wishes to consult her pocket notebook.

In relation to refreshing memory, which of the following is true?

A She cannot refer to her pocket notebook as she made the notes in consultation.

B She cannot refer to her pocket notebook as she refreshed her memory prior to giving evidence.

C She can refer to her pocket notebook, but only for exact details, i.e. index numbers.

D She can refer to her pocket notebook, provided she states that it records her recollection of the case.

Question 3.3

PERKINS has received a summons for a motoring offence and intends to plead guilty by post. PERKINS has previous motoring convictions within the last three years.

In relation to these previous convictions and pleading guilty by post, which of the following is correct?

A If the court wishes to use the previous convictions, they must give the accused notice of that intention but allow the guilty plea by post.

B If the court wishes to use the previous convictions, they must give the accused notice of that intention and direct the accused attend in person.

C The court can use the previous convictions without giving the accused notice of that intention, but can only use a certified court record of those convictions.

D The court can use the previous convictions without giving the accused notice of that intention, and can use a DVLA printout to do so.

Question 3.4

Police are investigating a number of sexual offences at a residential home where most of the occupants have impaired intellect. Charges have been raised and there are a number of victims and witnesses who have severe learning difficulties. A determination has to be made as to whether such a witness is competent to give intelligible testimony under s. 55 of the Youth Justice and Criminal Evidence Act 1999.

In relation to this, which of the following will the court consider?

A Whether the witness understands the oath and can respond to any questions posed.

B Whether the witness is acceptable to both the prosecution and defence counsel.

C Whether the witness is able to understand questions put to him/her and is fit to attend trial.

D Whether the witness is able to understand questions put to him/her and give answers to them which can be understood.

Question 3.5

CONVOY is a witness to a theft of petrol committed by her husband and she is being interviewed by the police who are investigating the theft. They do not tell her that she is not a compellable witness and, although she is reluctant, she gives a statement. She is called to court but refuses to give evidence against her husband and the judge rules that she is not compellable. The prosecution seeks to admit the wife's statement under s. 114 of the Criminal Justice Act 2003.

Can her statement be admitted as evidence?

A Yes, as her statement was not obtained fraudulently by the police, she didn't ask if she had to make it.

B Yes, as there is no requirement to tell a wife that she is not compellable prior to obtaining a statement.

C No, the police are required to tell a witness that they cannot be compelled to give evidence where in law they cannot be so compelled.

D No, as the police are aware that she is reluctant to give a statement they must tell her that she cannot be compelled.

Question 3.6

DYER is appearing at Crown Court on a charge of burglary having originally pleaded not guilty at magistrates' court and electing to be indicted. However, fearing a prison sentence, he changes his plea to guilty prior to any evidence being adduced. One matter of concern for DYER is that the prosecution maintains that the burglary involved the theft of an expensive oil painting—DYER admits stealing a painting but states that it was a fake and not as valuable as the prosecution maintains.

What evidence should the prosecution now call?

A Only the accused's criminal record.

B Only the accused's antecedents and criminal record, he has pleaded guilty.

C The accused's antecedents and criminal record and where necessary evidence to support its version of the facts.

D Only evidence that supports the prosecution version of the facts.

Question 3.7

GRAINGER is 40 years of age and is accused of criminal damage and due to appear at magistrates' court (by way of a summons); however, he has failed to appear. The court is satisfied that the summons was served in the prescribed manner. There is no notice given by GRAINGER as to why he is not there.

In relation to this, which of the following is correct?

A The court should inquire as to why GRAINGER is not present; if no satisfactory answer is received, it should proceed in his absence.

B The court should consider whether it should issue a warrant for GRAINGER's arrest or issue a summons compelling him to attend.

C The court may proceed in his absence unless it appears to the court to be contrary to the interests of justice to do so.

D The court must proceed in his absence unless it appears to the court to be contrary to the interests of justice to do so.

Question 3.8

POLE is a witness to an offence of theft which also involved injury to the victim. Although POLE told officers investigating the incident exactly what he saw and made a witness statement in relation to the incident, POLE refuses to attend court and give evidence. The prosecution tells the magistrates' court, where the defendant is being tried, what evidence POLE can give, that it is material evidence and that it would be in the interests of justice to issue a summons to obtain POLE's attendance at the court to give evidence.

Considering the power of the court to secure POLE's attendance to provide evidence, which of the following statements is correct?

A In such a situation, the court cannot issue a summons, warrant or order to secure POLE's attendance; this power is only available to cases tried in the Crown Court.

B Where a witness is summoned but refuses to give evidence or answer questions, he/she may be dealt with for perverting the course of justice.

C If a summons is issued, it must be served personally by handing it to POLE.

D If appropriate, such an application by the prosecution could be used as a preemptive measure to secure the attendance of POLE at the court.

Question 3.9

PRICE witnessed an offence of robbery and gave an oral account of what she witnessed to PC FREETH who made an audio recording of PRICE's account; the audio recording was later transcribed. Several months later, BOYD was arrested and charged with the offence and the case has come to trial at Crown Court. PRICE is waiting to give evidence but is nervous in case she forgets anything as a significant amount of time had passed between the oral account being given by PRICE and the case coming to court. PRICE asks PC FREETH if she can refresh her memory from the transcript of her oral account before she goes into the witness box; PC FREETH allows her to read the transcript.

In relation to refreshing memory, which of the comments below is correct?

A PC FREETH should have allowed PRICE to listen to the audio recording he made and not allowed her to read the transcript.

B PRICE could refresh her memory of the matter from the transcript when giving oral evidence in the Crown Court.

C PRICE could not refresh her memory from the transcript when giving witness evidence in the Crown Court as she had refreshed her memory from the transcript outside the Crown Court.

D A witness may only refresh their memory from an account made or verified by him/her at an earlier time which was written down at the time the account was given.

Question 3.10

Section 80 of the Police and Criminal Evidence Act 1984 (as amended by the Youth Justice and Criminal Evidence Act 1999) details circumstances when a wife, husband or civil partner is compellable to give evidence against their spouse or civil partner.

In which of the following circumstances would the named person be compellable to give evidence on behalf of the prosecution against their spouse or civil partner?

A JOHN and ALAN are civil partners (by virtue of the Civil Partnership Act 2004). During an argument in the street, JOHN threatened to injure ALAN. JOHN is charged with an offence of affray (contrary to s. 3 of the Public Order Act 1986).

B JILL and PAUL are married. JILL witnesses PAUL commit an offence of assault by penetration (contrary to s. 2 of the Sexual Offences Act 2003) against a person who, at the time of the assault, was 16 years old.

C FRANK and JULIE are married. FRANK witnesses JULIE commit an offence of grievous bodily harm with intent (contrary to s. 18 of the Offences Against the Person Act 1861) against a person who, at the time of the assault, was 19 years old.

D KATE and MARY are civil partners (by virtue of the Civil Partnership Act 2004). KATE steals £3,000 from MARY's private bank account.

Question 3.11

KENTSLEY (aged 25 years) commits a s. 47 assault (contrary to the Offences Against the Person Act 1861) and is summonsed to appear at a magistrates' court in respect of the matter. However, at the time and place appointed for KENTSLEY's trial for the offence, KENTSLEY does not appear.

Could KENTSLEY's trial for the offence go ahead in the magistrates' court in these circumstances?

A No, the only option the court has is to issue a warrant for the accused's arrest under s. 7 of the Bail Act 1976.

B Yes, but this is only because KENTSLEY is over 18 years of age, as if he were under 18 years of age the case could not proceed in his absence.

C No, the court must either issue a warrant for the accused's arrest under s. 7 of the Bail Act 1976 or appoint a later time when the accused has to appear in accordance with s. 129(3) of the Magistrates' Courts Act 1980.

D Yes, but the court must be satisfied that the summons was served in a prescribed manner before commencing in KENTSLEY's absence.

Question 3.12

CURTIN has been charged with an offence of kidnapping and has pleaded 'not guilty' to the offence which will be tried in Crown Court. STILWELL is a vital prosecution witness but was involved in an accident 200 miles away from the Crown Court and cannot physically get to the Crown Court to give his evidence due to the injuries he received in the accident. However, STILWELL can get to a location near the hospital where he is being treated which will enable him to provide his evidence through a 'live link'.

Could the court authorise that STILWELL be allowed to provide his evidence via a live link with consideration to the Criminal Justice Act 2003?

A The court would not be able to authorise STILWELL to provide his evidence in this manner as the use of live link is restricted to trials of serious sexual offences.

B The court may authorise the use of a live link if it has considered all the circumstances of the case, including the importance of the witness's evidence to the proceedings.

C The court would not be able to authorise STILWELL to give his evidence in this manner unless he was outside the United Kingdom at the time of the trial.

D The court may authorise the use of a live link but only because this is an indictable offence being tried in the Crown Court.

Question 3.13

PERRY is a victim in a case of rape and is due to attend trial at Crown Court. PERRY is concerned that the defendant—SHARP—may seek to have questions asked of her with respect to her previous sexual behaviour and experiences.

With regards to s. 42(1) of the Youth Justice and Criminal Evidence Act, which of the following is correct?

A Questions may be asked of the complainant but only if they are relevant in order to confirm previous experiences.

B Questions may not be asked of the complainant unless they are with the agreement of both prosecution and defence.

C Questions may be asked of the complainant but only if they are linked to previous relevant complaints.

D Questions may not be asked of the complainant by or on behalf of an accused.

ANSWERS

Answer 3.1

Answer **A** — In the Crown Court the prosecution must appear by legal representative but the accused may still conduct his/her own case. An accused conducting his/her own case may be allowed a friend to accompany him/her as an adviser though such an adviser may not question witnesses or address the court (*McKenzie* v *McKenzie* [1970] 3 WLR 472), making answers B, C and D incorrect.

Evidence and Procedure, para. 2.3.5

Answer 3.2

Answer **D** — Section 139 of the Criminal Justice Act 2003 states:

(1) A person giving oral evidence in criminal proceedings about any matter may, at any stage in the course of doing so, refresh his memory of it from a document made or verified by him at an earlier time if—
   (a) he states in his oral evidence that the document records his recollection of the matter at that earlier time, and
   (b) his recollection of the matter is likely to have been significantly better at that time than it is at the time of his oral evidence.

So the officer can refer to her notebook, irrespective of any factors under which such notes were made, if she states it is her recollection, and such recollection is likely to be significantly better than it is now whilst giving evidence-in-chief. Answers A, B and C are therefore incorrect.

Evidence and Procedure, para. 2.3.10

Answer 3.3

Answer **D** — The procedure for a defendant to plead guilty by post is provided by the Magistrates' Courts Act 1980 and applies to proceedings for summary offences started by way of summons (or requisition) in the magistrates' court (s. 12(1)), or in the youth court for persons aged 16 or 17 (s. 12(2)). The summons (or requisition) is served on the defendant together with a 'statement of facts' and a prescribed form of explanation. This allows the defendant an opportunity to plead guilty and put forward any mitigation in his/her absence. The magistrates' designated officer informs the prosecution of any written guilty plea.

This section is most commonly used for driving offences and provision is made for a printout from the DVLA to be admissible as evidence of previous convictions for traffic offences without the need to give an accused notice of intention to refer to these previous convictions (s. 13 of the Road Traffic Offenders Act 1988); answers A, B and C are therefore incorrect.

Evidence and Procedure, para. 2.3.2

Answer 3.4

Answer **D** — The law in relation to witnesses with a disorder or disability of the mind is contained in s. 55 of the Youth Justice and Criminal Evidence Act 1999.

In determining whether such a witness is competent to give *intelligible testimony*, expert evidence is allowed, or the court may consider whether the witness is able to understand questions put to him/her and give answers to them which can be understood; answers A, B and C are therefore incorrect.

Evidence and Procedure, para. 2.3.7.8

Answer 3.5

Answer **B** — A wife, husband or civil partner is only compellable to give evidence on behalf of the prosecution against his/her spouse or partner (unless jointly charged) in certain circumstances. A charge of theft would not be one of those circumstances— so in this scenario the wife *would not* be a compellable witness. In *R* v *L* [2008] EWCA Crim 973, the court held that there is no requirement to tell a wife that she is not a compellable witness against her husband before interviewing her about a crime of which her husband is suspected; answers C and D are therefore incorrect. A statement obtained from the wife in such circumstances could be admitted in evidence even though the wife refused to give evidence against her husband, provided it did not lead to an injustice. This is irrespective of whether the wife asks or not; answer A is therefore incorrect.

Evidence and Procedure, para. 2.3.7.5

Answer 3.6

Answer **C** — Where there is a 'guilty plea', which must be entered personally by the accused (*R* v *Ellis* (1973) 57 Cr App R 571), the only evidence which the prosecution needs to call are details of the accused's antecedents and criminal record (answers A and D are therefore incorrect). Where it is necessary, where there is disagreement about the precise facts of the offence, the prosecution may be required to call evidence to support its version of the facts, known as *Newton* hearings (*R* v *Newton* (1983) 77 Cr App R 13); answer B is therefore incorrect.

Evidence and Procedure, para. 2.3.5

Answer 3.7

Answer **D** — Where an accused fails to appear in the magistrates' court in answer to bail the court may:

- issue a warrant for the accused's arrest under s. 7 of the Bail Act 1976;
- appoint a later time when the accused has to appear in accordance with s. 129(3) of the Magistrates' Courts Act 1980;
- proceed in the accused's absence under s. 11(1) of the Magistrates' Courts Act 1980.

Where the accused's appearance was by way of summons, the court must be satisfied that the summons was served in the prescribed manner before commencing in the accused's absence (s. 11(2)).

Where an accused is under 18 years of age, the court may proceed in his/her absence (s. 11(1)(a) of the 1980 Act) and, if the accused has attained the age of 18, the court must proceed in his/her absence unless it appears to the court to be contrary to the interests of justice do so (s. 11(1)(b)); answers B and C are therefore incorrect.

The court is not required to inquire into the reasons for the accused's failure to appear (s. 11(6))—answer A is therefore incorrect—but where it imposes a custodial sentence the accused must be brought before the court before commencing a custodial sentence (s. 11(3A)).

Evidence and Procedure, para. 2.3.6

Answer 3.8

Answer **D** — The prosecution or the defence can apply for a summons, warrant or order requiring a witness to attend a magistrates' court (s. 97 or 97A of the Magistrates' Courts Act 1980, or para. 4 of sch. 3 to the Crime and Disorder Act 1998), making answer A incorrect. Answer B is incorrect as where such a summons is issued and the witness refuses to give evidence or answer questions, the witness may be dealt with for contempt of court (not pervert the course of justice—pervert the course of justice is a 'positive' act offence, i.e. the defendant must actually do something rather than fail to give evidence or answer questions which is an omission). A witness summons is served by handing it to the individual, or leaving it at or posting it to an address where it is reasonably believed the witness will receive it (Criminal Procedure Rules 2014), and this makes answer C incorrect. Issuing a summons can be used as a pre-emptive measure. The procedure for the service of a witness summons is contained in the Magistrates' Courts (Amendment) Rules 2019, r. 99(1)(a) to (k).

Evidence and Procedure, para. 2.3.7.1

Answer 3.9

Answer **B** — Section 139 of the Criminal Justice Act 2003 states that where a person giving oral evidence in criminal proceedings about any matter has previously given an oral account, of which a sound recording was made, and the witness states in that evidence that the account represents his/her recollection at the time and that his/her recollection of the matter is likely to have been significantly better at the time of the previous account than it is at the time of their oral evidence and that a transcript has been made of the sound recording, he/she may, at any stage in the course of giving his/her evidence, refresh his/her memory of the matter from that transcript (s. 139(2)) (making answers A and D incorrect). The same rule applies to an account that was written down at the time, e.g. a written statement (s. 139(1)). Answer C is incorrect as the presumption made under s. 139(2) is applicable whether the witness refreshed his/her memory from a document or transcript before going into the witness box.

Evidence and Procedure, para. 2.3.10

Answer 3.10

Answer **A** — A wife, husband or civil partner is only compellable to give evidence on behalf of the prosecution in certain circumstances. Answer B is not one of those as the sexual offence the wife witnessed would need to be committed on a person who at the time of the offence was *under* 16 years of age. Answer C is incorrect as, once again, the victim of the assault/injury would need to be under 16 years of age at the material time. Answer D is incorrect as theft is not an offence covered by this legislation.

Evidence and Procedure, para. 2.3.7.5

Answer 3.11

Answer **D** — Answer D is correct as where the accused's appearance was by way of summons, the court must be satisfied that the summons was served in a prescribed manner (s. 11(2) of the Magistrates' Courts Act 1980). Where an accused fails to appear in the magistrates' court in answer to bail, the court may:

- issue a warrant for the accused's arrest under s. 7 of the Bail Act 1976 (see para. 2.2.10);
- appoint a later time when the accused has to appear in accordance with s. 129(3) of the Magistrates' Courts Act 1980;
- proceed in the accused's absence under s. 11(1) of the Magistrates' Courts Act 1980.

Any one of the above could be selected by the court so this makes answers A and C incorrect. Where an accused is under 18 years of age, the court *may* proceed in his/her absence (s. 11(1)(a)), making answer B incorrect.

Evidence and Procedure, para. 2.3.6

Answer 3.12

Answer **B** — Answer A is incorrect as 'live link' evidence is not restricted to a witness giving evidence in a trial in relation to a serious sexual offence—it can be given in any eligible criminal proceedings. 'Eligible criminal proceedings' include a preliminary hearing, a summary trial and a trial on indictment or any other trial in the Crown Court for an offence (as outlined in the Criminal Justice Act 2003, s. 51(3)). The fact that it can be given in any trial also means that answer D is incorrect. Section 32(1) of the Criminal Justice Act 1988 allows for 'live link' evidence from witnesses outside the United Kingdom to be authorised—s. 51 of the Criminal Justice Act 2003 allows the same process within the United Kingdom, meaning that answer C is incorrect. Answer B is correct as the court, when giving the direction, must consider all the circumstances of the case, including the importance of the witness's evidence to the proceedings. It must also consider whether the direction might tend to inhibit any party to the proceedings from effectively testing the witness's evidence, and the arrangements that would or could be put in place for members of the public to see or hear the proceedings as conducted in accordance with the direction (Criminal Justice Act 2003, s. 56(6)).

Evidence and Procedure, para. 2.3.8.1

Answer 3.13

Answer **D** — The Youth Justice and Criminal Evidence Act 1999 provides that where a person is charged with a sexual offence no evidence may be adduced and no questions asked in cross-examination by or on behalf of an accused about any sexual behaviour of the complainant (s. 41(1)). 'Sexual behaviour' means any sexual behaviour or other sexual experience, whether or not involving any accused or other person, but excluding anything alleged to have taken place which is the subject matter of the charge against the accused (s. 42(1)(c)). It may refer to acts or events of a sexual character, as opposed to the existence of a relationship, acquaintanceship or familiarity. The phrases are wide enough to embrace the viewing of pornography, or sexually charged messaging over a live internet connection or answering questions in a sexually implicit quiz (*R* v *Ben-Rejab* [2011] EWCA Crim 1136). However, in *R* v *T* [2021] EWCA Crim 318, it was held that evidence or questioning about the complainant's sexual behaviour which involves speculation or is simply irrelevant to any issues in the case is inadmissible. The provisions of the 1999 Act recognise that to allow victims of sexual offences to be harassed unfairly by questions about their previous sexual experiences is unjust to them and bad for society, because if victims are afraid to complain then the guilty may escape justice. Therefore A, B and C are incorrect.

Evidence and Procedure, para. 2.3.14.2

4 | Exclusion of Admissible Evidence

QUESTIONS

Question 4.1

WILLIAMS and THOMPSON were jointly charged with possessing stolen property. In his police interview, WILLIAMS admitted that he knew the goods were stolen but stated that THOMPSON had no knowledge of that. WILLIAMS pleaded guilty. THOMPSON pleaded not guilty and at his trial argued that he did not know that the property amounted to stolen goods. WILLIAMS indicated he would be unwilling to give evidence at court on behalf of THOMPSON and was therefore not called by the defence. Instead, the defence sought to rely on WILLIAMS's statements in his police interview.

Will this previous confession by WILLIAMS be admissible in THOMPSON's trial?

A Yes, the statement will be allowed as he is no longer a defendant, he is only a witness.

B Yes, the statement will be allowed as a confession made by one accused person can be given in evidence for another person charged in the same proceedings.

C No, the statement will not be allowed as WILLIAMS is no longer charged in the same proceedings.

D No, the statement won't be allowed as the confession was from WILLIAMS not from THOMPSON and is therefore inadmissible.

Question 4.2

FRENCH is standing trial at the Crown Court, charged with blackmail. The defence ask the judge to exclude certain evidence that the prosecution seeks to adduce exercising common law powers retained by s. 82(3) of the Police and Criminal Evidence Act 1984.

For evidence to be excluded at common law, the court will do what?

A Concern itself with the effect that the evidence will have at trial rather than how the evidence was obtained.

B Concern itself with how the evidence was obtained rather than the effect that the evidence will have at trial.

C Concern itself with how the evidence was obtained and in particular whether there have been any breaches of the Codes of Practice.

D Concern itself with how the evidence was presented during the trial considering what effect that evidence will have on the trial.

Question 4.3

TIMPKINS was arrested for murder. He was told by the interviewing officer that if he confessed he would probably be charged with manslaughter at the worst; TIMPKINS consequently stated that he had shot the victim in self-defence. TIMPKINS then told the officers where to find the gun, which he had hidden in a hedge. The gun was found, and at a second interview TIMPKINS identified it as the one he had used, again because he believed he would be charged with manslaughter only. Ballistic evidence showed it was the weapon used. TIMPKINS was charged with murder. At TIMPKINS's trial, the judge ruled that the confession obtained at the first interview would be excluded as it was 'unreliable'.

In relation to evidence the police can now give, which of the following statements is true?

A The police can state that TIMPKINS identified the gun, as this was during the second interview, which should be allowed.

B The police can state that they found a gun where TIMPKINS told them to look, and that it was the gun used in the shooting.

C The police may not be able to make a connection between TIMPKINS and the gun.

D The police will be able to state that TIMPKINS said he had used the gun, as this was during the second interview, which should be allowed.

Question 4.4

VENTHAM was suspected by his employers of stealing from work colleagues and was interviewed by the employers. He was told that if he admitted that he had been stealing he would be sacked but that the police would not be contacted. If he denied the thefts, the police would be called to investigate. He told his employer that he had stolen and they contacted the police anyway. He was charged with theft and his 'confession' was sought to be adduced in evidence against him.

Would VENTHAM's confession to his employers be allowed in evidence?

A No, this confession would not be allowed as it was not made to a person in authority and is therefore inadmissible.

B No, this confession would not be allowed as it would be deemed to be unreliable due to the inducement to make it.

C Yes, this confession would be allowed as the inducement was not made by a person in authority and therefore would be admissible.

D Yes, the confession would be allowed provided VENTHAM was asked about it during a formal police interview as a significant statement.

Question 4.5

BLOUNT left explicit graffiti messages in a public lavatory, seeking sex with girls aged between 8 and 13 years, and asking them to follow him on Twitter, leaving his Twitter name. The police became aware and monitored his social media account. With the relevant authority, a police officer followed BLOUNT on Twitter and sent several messages implying that she was a 12-year-old girl, and interested in meeting him. BLOUNT replied, arranging a meeting and describing the various sexual acts he would perform on her. At the meeting, he was arrested and later charged with attempting to incite a child under the age of 13 to engage in sexual activity, contrary to s. 8 of the Sexual Offences Act 2003.

Would the activity of the police in this situation be considered to be 'entrapment'?

A No, as the police provided no more than an opportunity to commit the offence.

B No, the police action was no more than an attempt to locate and arrest him.

C Yes, as the officer purporting to be the child was not under 13 years of age, the offence could never be committed.

D Yes, as the police operated using a false persona and therefore this would be entrapment.

Question 4.6

BARKER and JONES were both suspected of committing a murder. During police interviews they exercised their right to silence. There was other evidence and they were charged. The senior investigating officer (SIO) was concerned that the evidence was flimsy and wanted confession evidence from the suspects. Aware that no further interviews were allowed, the SIO concocted a ruse where the custody officer argued with the SIO in front of the suspects claiming he had to place them both in the same cell. The SIO apologised to the suspects claiming that the custody officer was an 'arse for making you share a cell'. The cell was bugged and the suspects engaged in a conversation which contained a number of damaging admissions, and was recorded.

Would the recorded admissions in the cell be admissible in evidence?

A Yes, the evidence is admissible as the police did not trick them into making the admissions.

B Yes, the evidence will be admissible but the police will have to re-interview them to allow them to comment upon it.

C No, the evidence is not admissible as it was obtained after interview and charge.

D No, the evidence is not admissible as it was obtained by a cheat, where the custody officer clearly lied to the suspects.

Question 4.7

LARK is an undercover officer working on a drugs operation. The police are carrying out an operation on XANTHOS, a known drug dealer. LARK is authorised (proper authorities for this operation have been obtained) to purchase drugs from XANTHOS. He approaches XANTHOS who offers to sell him a wrap of amphetamine. LARK hands over the money and takes the drugs. During the transaction, LARK asks XANTHOS if he can supply a firearm for a robbery he is planning. XANTHOS agrees to this and plans a later meeting.

In relation to LARK's request, which of the following is true?

A This is not entrapment as XANTHOS is volunteering to get the firearm.

B This is not entrapment as the undercover operation has been authorised.

C This may be entrapment as LARK is no longer a passive observer.

D This is entrapment as LARK was not authorised by the operation to buy firearms.

Question 4.8

BOVELL is arrested for an offence of sexual assault. She is interviewed and during the interview she confesses to the offence. BOVELL is charged with sexual assault and the case goes to trial, where BOVELL pleads not guilty to the offence, alleging that her confession was obtained by oppression and in circumstances that would render it unreliable.

Which of the following statements is correct?

A BOVELL's 'confession' evidence can only be excluded under s. 76 of the Police and Criminal Evidence Act 1984.

B The only way evidence can be excluded during the trial is under ss. 76 and 78 of the Police and Criminal Evidence Act.

C BOVELL's 'confession' falls into the category of evidence known as 'hearsay' evidence.

D Once the issue of oppression and/or unreliability is raised, it is for the defence to prove that the confession was obtained in such circumstances.

Question 4.9

DC WILES is mentoring PC COOMBS who is on attachment to CID during his probationary period and they are about to go into an interview with TAYLOR who is in custody in relation to an allegation of assault. PC COOMBS asks DC WILES what would amount to 'oppression' in relation to s. 76(8) of the Police and Criminal Evidence Act 1984.

Which of the following would be the correct answer from DC WILES?

A Where the Codes of Practice have been followed, there can never be any 'oppression'.

B It might be possible for the defence to use evidence against officers involved in a case who have allegedly 'mistreated' suspects in other cases.

C The 'oppression' does not necessarily have to be against the person who makes the confession.

D A failure to follow the Codes of Practice will automatically lead to the exclusion of evidence on the grounds of 'oppression'.

Question 4.10

FAZAL is in custody in relation to historic child sexual offences and makes significant confessions to his appropriate adult, GILL, whilst at the police station. These confessions were made by FAZAL unprompted by GILL, who was an unwilling recipient, and were subsequently used in evidence at trial resulting in his conviction.

In relation to s. 76(2)(b) of the Police and Criminal Evidence Act 1984, would these circumstances tender the confession as unreliable?

A Yes, because a confession volunteered by anyone requiring an appropriate adult will always be unreliable in line with s. 76(2)(b).

B No, because a confession volunteered without anything being said or done cannot fall foul of s. 76(2)(b).

C Yes, because any confession volunteered regardless of anything being said or done may fall foul of s. 76(2)(b).

D No, because it is for the prosecution to show reliability only if argued by the defence in line with s. 76(2)(b).

ANSWERS

Answer 4.1

Answer **C** — In ensuring that a person has a fair trial, the court may exclude evidence, even though the evidence itself is admissible. The court may exclude any evidence in certain circumstances and has additional powers in relation to evidence obtained by confession. The courts' powers to exclude evidence come generally from s. 78 of the Police and Criminal Evidence Act 1984 (and specifically in relation to confession evidence from s. 76(2) of that Act), although the courts also have common law powers to exclude evidence.

This is supported by s. 76A of the Police and Criminal Evidence Act 1984 which states that as long as it has not been excluded by the court under s. 76A (which makes similar provisions for exclusion as those under s. 76), in any proceedings where a confession was made by one accused person it may be given in evidence for another person charged in the same proceedings (a co-accused); answer D is therefore incorrect.

The key part of this subsection is that the co-accused must be 'charged in the same proceedings', for instance in *R v Finch* [2007] EWCA Crim 36 where one suspect pleaded guilty the House of Lords held that he was no longer a person charged or accused in the trial, accordingly s. 76A of the 1984 Act did not apply and what he said to the police was not admissible; answer B is therefore incorrect.

It is correct to say that he is a witness, however, he would have to give evidence-in-chief, and a previous confession made on tape would NOT be admissible as outlined in *Finch*; answer A is therefore incorrect.

Evidence and Procedure, para. 2.4.2

Answer 4.2

Answer **A** — Section 82(3) of the Police and Criminal Evidence Act 1984 retained the courts' common law power to exclude evidence at their discretion (as to which, see *R v Sang* [1980] AC 402). For evidence to be excluded at common law, the court will not so much concern itself with *how* evidence is obtained, but rather the *effect* that the evidence will have at trial; answer B is therefore incorrect as this reverses that doctrine.

Evidence can be excluded at common law at any time during the trial, including pre-trial submissions (*voir dire*) so it can be excluded prior to evidence even being presented; answer D is therefore incorrect.

In these cases, the courts are looking at the trial process itself as opposed to the investigation, and therefore this power has less impact on how investigations should be conducted therefore breaches of the Codes of Practice have limited effect here; answer C is therefore incorrect.

Evidence and Procedure, para. 2.4.3.4

Answer 4.3

Answer **C** — This question shows what could happen where vital evidence is lost due to police impropriety (i.e. a clear inducement to confess), particularly where a false pretence has been used. The first interview was rightly excluded, and for the same reasons it is more than likely that the second interview would also be excluded. Answers A and D are therefore incorrect. In this case, it will not be possible to show any connection between the suspect and the weapon and, unless there is some other evidence to link the weapon to the suspect, the case may fail. The reason is that it would not be possible to say that the police went to the location where the weapon was hidden without at least implying that the suspect had indicated that it was there when interviewed, and answer B is therefore incorrect. All that can be said is that the weapon was found at the particular location, which could be accessible to any number of people, and that the scientific evidence shows it to be the murder weapon.

Evidence and Procedure, para. 2.4.2.7

Answer 4.4

Answer **B** — A 'confession' is defined by s. 82 of the 1984 Act, which states:

> In this Part of this Act—'confession' includes any statement wholly or partly adverse to the person who made it, whether made to a person in authority or not and whether made in words or otherwise...

So a confession can be made to a person not in authority; answer A is therefore incorrect.

Is the confession reliable and admissible? A defendant was told by his employer that if he admitted to the theft no further action would be taken, but if he did not admit it, the employer would contact the police. The suspect admitted it; nevertheless the employer called the police. The manager's untrue inducement to the defendant made his confession unreliable, therefore the confession had been wrongfully admitted, which rendered the conviction unsafe (*R* v *Roberts* [2011] EWCA Crim 2974). The promise not to involve the police held out by a shop manager to an employee suspected of stealing gave rise to the inference that anything said in consequence was likely to be unreliable; answer C is therefore incorrect.

A significant statement is one which appears to be capable of being used in evidence, and in particular a direct admission of guilt, so as this statement could not be used (as per *Roberts*), answer D is incorrect.

Evidence and Procedure, paras 2.4.2, 2.4.2.6

Answer 4.5

Answer **A** — The issue of entrapment falls into two categories: that is to say, trying to obtain evidence relating to offences that have already been committed and those cases where evidence is obtained of offences yet to be committed. In relation to offences yet to be committed, the key question is whether the suspects voluntarily applied themselves to 'the trick' and that they were not enticed or provoked into committing a crime which they would otherwise not have committed. In *R* v *Jones* [2007] EWCA Crim 1118, the police had received reports of graffiti being written in black marker in the toilets of trains and stations seeking girls of 8 to 13 years old for sex, offering payment and leaving a contact number. In *Jones*, police began an undercover operation using an officer posing as a 12-year-old girl. The undercover officer exchanged several texts with the suspect which clarified her age and arrangements for a meeting. The defendant sent the officer further text messages of an explicit nature including various sexual acts that he expected he would be able to perform on her. The Court of Appeal held that the police did not incite or instigate a crime but merely provided the opportunity for the defendant to commit a similar offence and provide evidence for a conviction. The fact that the officer is acting with a false persona on a social media site is acceptable with the relevant authorisation; answer D is therefore incorrect. The officer did no more than pretend to be a child of a particular age. The police did not behave improperly in choosing the age of 12. In the scenario of this question, it was BLOUNT who had asked the officer for her age, and he therefore believed that he was inciting penetrative sexual activity with a child under 13.

BLOUNT is charged with an attempt to commit the offence, and the message in the toilet would not be 'more than merely preparatory'; however, the police action is certainly more than an attempt just to locate him, and is part of evidence gathering;

for these reasons, answer B is incorrect. As the offence charged is 'attempt', it is irrelevant that the actual offence could not have been committed; answer C is therefore incorrect.

Evidence and Procedure, para. 2.4.4

Answer 4.6

Answer **A** — In *R* v *Bailey* [1993] 3 All ER 513, a blatant piece of play-acting was approved. The investigating officers and the custody officer played out a conversation in front of the defendants, in which the custody officer, appearing to act against the wishes of the investigating officers, insisted on placing the two defendants in the same cell. In fact, the investigating officers wanted the defendants together, as the cell was bugged. The defendants, lulled into a false sense of security, engaged in a conversation which contained a number of damaging admissions, and was recorded. The Court of Appeal found nothing wrong in what the police had done, even though it was clearly a means of circumventing the fact that they could not question the defendants further (because they had both already been charged). The court held that the fact the defendants could not, under Code of Practice C, properly have been subjected to further questioning did not mean that they had to be protected from the opportunity to speak incriminatingly to one another if they chose to do so. It was acknowledged to appear odd that, alongside the rigorously controlled legislative regime for questioning, it should be considered acceptable for covert investigations legitimately to continue but, provided such stratagems were used only in grave cases and that there was no suggestion of oppression or unreliability, there was nothing unfair about admitting the evidence obtained in consequence.

The evidence will be adduced; answers B, C and D are therefore incorrect.

Evidence and Procedure, para. 2.4.4

Answer 4.7

Answer **D** — Police entrapment occurs when a law enforcer such as a police constable causes a person to commit an offence with the intention of prosecution for that offence. (For example, posing or hiring someone to pose as a street prostitute and waiting for a 'kerb crawler' to attempt to solicit for the services of the prostitute from their vehicle.) Therefore, the key issue in an application for a stay of proceedings on the grounds of abuse of process or exclusion of evidence under s. 78 of the Police and Criminal Evidence Act 1984 in entrapment cases is the conduct of the police or the prosecuting authority. There has to be some kind of criticism to be levelled specifically at the police or the Crown Prosecution Service relating to how the evidence was obtained; without this impropriety, any argument regarding exclusion of evidence or an abuse of process is likely to fail. In this scenario, the criticism is that the officer went beyond the brief for the operation and therefore it was an abuse of process. Sometimes the lines can be blurred in these cases as to what is or is not entrapment; in this scenario, however, the abuse of process is clear—the officer has asked the suspect to commit an offence completely unrelated to the operation the officer is undercover for and such is clear entrapment; answers A, B and C are therefore incorrect.

Evidence and Procedure, para. 2.4.4

Answer 4.8

Answer **C** — Answer A is incorrect as confession evidence can be excluded under s. 78 as well as s. 76 of the Police and Criminal Evidence Act 1984. Answer B is incorrect as evidence can also be excluded under s. 82(1) of the Act that preserves the court's common law power to exclude evidence at its discretion. Answer D is incorrect as once the defence raises the issue of oppression or unreliability, it is for the prosecution to prove the confession was not obtained in such circumstances (*R* v *Allen* [2001] EWCA Crim 1607). The burden of proof will be beyond all reasonable doubt.

Evidence and Procedure, paras 2.4.1, 2.4.2.1, 2.4.3.2

Answer 4.9

Answer **B** — A failure to follow the Codes of Practice is not an automatic reason for excluding evidence, making answer D incorrect. Answer C is incorrect as the oppression must have been against the person who made the confession. Answer A is incorrect as there can be 'oppressive' behaviour even though the Codes of Practice have been followed.

Evidence and Procedure, para. 2.4.2.4

Answer 4.10

Answer **B** — Under s. 76(2)(b) of the Police and Criminal Evidence Act 1984, a court is under a duty to exclude a confession where it is, has been or may have been obtained in consequence of anything which was likely, in the circumstances that existed at the time, to render it unreliable.

When looking at whether a confession is reliable, the court will consider the circumstances as they actually were at the time and not as they were believed to be. For instance, if it was believed that a suspect was in a fit state to be interviewed but it later transpires that he/she was medically unfit, there is likely to be some doubt as to whether a confession made at that time is reliable. (The belief of the officers at the time of acting, however, may be relevant to any disciplinary matters.)

A confession volunteered without anything being said or done cannot fall foul of s. 76(2)(b). In the case of *R v Ward* [2018] EWCA Crim 1464, an appeal against conviction was made for historic child sexual offences on the basis of the judge's failure to exclude the evidence of a confession made to an appropriate adult at the police station. Where the appropriate adult was the unwilling recipient of unsolicited confessions by an accused where nothing was said or done by the adult or anyone else, then it was unlikely to render the confession unreliable. Therefore answers A, C and D are incorrect.

Evidence and Procedure, para. 2.4.2.5

5 | Disclosure of Evidence

Question 5.1

Constable STEYN was investigating a fraud case, and had taken several statements. He spoke to one particular witness, ROGERS, who claimed that another witness, MURPHY, may not possibly have seen what she said she had seen. ROGERS claims MURPHY did not like the defendant as she had been rude to her previously. However, there is no evidence that MURPHY is lying in her statement and it's only ROGERS's opinion. The officer recorded this in his pocket notebook. All the statements taken indicate that the defendant passed cheques fraudulently and it was captured on CCTV.

Should the prosecution reveal the note in Constable STEYN's pocket notebook (as material that undermines the prosecution case)?

A No, as there is no evidence that MURPHY may be mistaken in what she saw, the note does not have to be disclosed.

B No, as there is other compelling evidence, including CCTV, this note does not have to be disclosed.

C Yes, the note would have to be disclosed as it relates to the investigation and has been recorded.

D Yes, the note would have to be disclosed as it indicates a possible motive for lying by a witness.

Question 5.2

Police officers have received intelligence to suggest that an armed robbery will take place at a local post office. They set up lawful surveillance on a post office, but after a day that is withdrawn as they have intelligence to suggest that HOUSE is the suspect and the surveillance moves on to him.

Regarding the surveillance at the post office, which of the following is correct in relation to material obtained during that surveillance in line with the Criminal Procedure and Investigations Act 1996 and its definition of 'criminal investigation'?

A All the material from the investigation/operation would need to be retained and disclosed if necessary, including the location of the surveillance.

B All the material from the investigation/operation would have to be reviewed to see if it is relevant to the defence case.

C All the material from the investigation/operation is not relevant as at that time a crime had not been committed.

D All the material from the investigation/operation is not relevant as at that time a suspect had not been identified.

Question 5.3

Police officers have been carrying out covert surveillance in relation to the large-scale supply of Class A drugs. They have used undercover officers and a CHIS (covert human intelligence source) and the undercover officers and the CHIS are clearly visible on the recorded footage. The defence has asked for this material, which was deemed to be sensitive by the prosecutor, to be made available to them.

In relation to this, which of the following is correct?

A The court would decide if 'public interest immunity' applied. If it did, the material need not be disclosed.

B As the material has been considered to be sensitive, it can only be disclosed if the 'public interest immunity' test fails or with the express written approval of the Attorney General.

C As the material has been considered to be sensitive, it can only be disclosed if the 'public interest immunity' test fails or with the express written approval of the Director of Public Prosecutions.

D The defence has an absolute right to disclosure of relevant evidence so the material should be made available to the defence.

Question 5.4

GREIG has been charged with an indictable offence and has been committed to Crown Court. The prosecution has provided initial disclosure. He intends calling a number of defence witnesses to give evidence at court.

In relation to these witnesses, which of the following is correct?

A The defence must indicate that it is calling witnesses other than the accused.

B The defence must provide details of any witnesses it intends to call at trial.

C The defence only has to indicate whether or not the defendant will be giving evidence.

D The defence is under no obligation to provide any details of defence witnesses.

Question 5.5

RICHLEY has been charged with an offence of fraud and the prosecution has given initial disclosure. The case will be tried in the Crown Court and the defence is preparing a defence statement.

Which of the following is correct in relation to what should be in that statement?

A Only the nature of the defence case is required at this stage.

B The nature of the defence case and any witnesses only.

C The nature of the defence case, witnesses and details of any alibi only.

D The nature of the defence case, witnesses, details of any alibi and any point of law to be raised.

Question 5.6

LICARI is giving evidence at the Crown Court as a prosecution witness. During LICARI's evidence-in-chief, she gives evidence which is materially inconsistent with the first statement she made earlier to the police. In her first statement to the police, LICARI stated that she had seen the accused at the place where the crime was committed about three hours before the crime was committed. This statement was contained in the schedule of unused material but was not disclosed by the prosecution as it did not undermine the prosecution's case. It is on her second statement to the police, which was disclosed, that she is now giving evidence.

What should the prosecution now do in relation to the first statement?

A Nothing, as disclosure rules ceased to apply when the trial began.

B Nothing, as the statement only supports the prosecution case, it does not undermine it.

C The prosecution should ensure it is retained in case of any future appeal.

D The prosecution should disclose it immediately so that the defence can use it in cross-examination to discredit the testimony of the witness.

Question 5.7

Detective Sergeant BARRY was the disclosure officer on a particularly complex fraud case; unfortunately, he broke his leg playing rugby and is unable to continue in his role as disclosure officer on the case. The case is nearing the stage where further disclosure is to be made.

At this stage, who is responsible for assigning a new disclosure officer?

A Detective Sergeant BARRY's supervisor.

B Detective Sergeant BARRY's supervisor or the police officer in charge of criminal investigations.

C Detective Sergeant BARRY's supervisor or the police officer in charge of criminal investigations in consultation with the Crown Prosecution Service.

D The prosecutor from the Crown Prosecution Service who is in direct charge of the investigation.

Question 5.8

During a police investigation into a street robbery, a key eye-witness provides a statement outlining in detail the description of the attacker. When the robber is eventually captured, he admits the offence in a recorded interview and there is ample supporting evidence to show he is guilty. The key eye-witness's description, however, is completely different from the actual appearance of the accused. The accused has indicated that he intends to plead guilty.

What does the Disclosure Code of Practice say in relation to whether this statement should be included on the schedule and disclosed?

A There would be no reason to disclose this as it does not undermine the prosecution case.

B There would be no reason to disclose this as it does not undermine the prosecution case and the accused had indicated a guilty plea.

C The material might assist the defence so should be disclosed if the disclosure officer thinks it meets this common law test.

D The material might assist the defence so should be disclosed if the prosecutor thinks it meets this common law test.

Question 5.9

The Criminal Procedure and Investigations Act 1996 outlines what statements should be disclosed in cases that involve complaints against police officers. ARPAN is the father of a youth who has made a complaint of assault against a police officer. He is aware that the police have obtained several witness statements.

In relation to these statements, which of the following is correct?

A ARPAN is entitled at any time to have those statements disclosed to him.

B ARPAN is entitled to have those statements disclosed to him at the conclusion of the investigation at the earliest.

C ARPAN is not entitled to any disclosure as he is not the actual complainant.

D ARPAN is only entitled to disclosure if criminal charges are raised against the police officer.

Question 5.10

EAST appeared in Crown Court as a defendant for an offence of robbery. Before the trial, EAST's solicitor served a defence statement on the prosecution, outlining an alibi for the offence, which the police were able to negate. EAST elected to give evidence on his own behalf during the trial and, under cross-examination, he put forward a different alibi to the offence. As a result, the prosecuting barrister sought permission from the court to examine EAST about the contents of his defence statement.

Could the prosecution's request be granted in these circumstances?

A No, under no circumstances can a defendant be cross-examined in relation to a defence statement.

B Yes, the request may be granted in these circumstances.

C No, a defendant may be cross-examined in relation to a defence statement only when he/she is accused of an offence of perjury.

D Yes, a defendant may be cross-examined in relation to a defence statement on every occasion.

Question 5.11

VESELY has been charged with an offence of causing death by dangerous driving and will be appearing before the Crown Court. The prosecution has given initial disclosure; and the defence provided a defence statement 22 days after the initial disclosure.

Which of the following is correct in relation to what the prosecution must now do?

A Consider the impact of the defence statement in terms of the need for any further disclosure as it was submitted in time.

B Consider the impact of the defence statement in terms of the need for any further disclosure, even though it was submitted outside the statutory 14-day period allowed.

C Consider the impact of the defence statement in terms of the need for any further disclosure, even though it was submitted outside the statutory 21-day period allowed.

D Consider the statement but, as it is late, the prosecution is no longer under an obligation to provide further disclosure; that is now voluntary.

Question 5.12

Numerous reports of drug dealing taking place outside a school have been received by the police. BUSBY, who is a resident of the street where the school is located, is so enraged by the behaviour of the drug dealers that he has told the police that they can use his house to carry out observations on the drug dealers. DS STENNETT is the officer in charge of the operation and she wishes to make sure that BUSBY's details will not be made public if a case in relation to the drug dealing were to reach a court.

Considering the ruling in R v Johnson [1988] 1 WLR 1377 and the advice relating to the minimum evidential requirements needed if disclosure is to be protected, which of the following comments is correct?

A Prior to a trial, a police officer of no lower rank than a superintendent must be able to testify that immediately prior to the trial they visited the place used for observations and ascertained the attitude of the occupiers to possible disclosure of the use previously made of the premises.

B The police officer in charge of the observations, no one of a lower rank than an inspector, must be able to testify that beforehand they visited the observation place and ascertained the attitude of the occupiers of the premises, not only as to their use, but to the possible disclosure which could lead to identification of the premises and the occupiers.

C Prior to a trial, a police officer of no lower rank than inspector must be able to testify that immediately prior to the trial they visited the place used for observations and ascertained the attitude of the occupiers to possible disclosure of the use previously made of the premises.

D The police officer in charge of the observations, no one of a lower rank than a sergeant, must be able to testify that beforehand they visited the observation place and ascertained the attitude of the occupiers of the premises, not only as to their use, but to the possible disclosure, which could lead to identification of the premises and the occupiers.

ANSWERS

Answer 5.1

Answer **D** — Disclosure by the prosecutor is covered by s. 3 of the Criminal Procedure and Investigations Act 1996. This section talks about material which 'might undermine the prosecution case against the accused'. Such material will consist mainly of material which raises questions over the strength of the prosecution case, the value of evidence given by witnesses and issues relating to identification. If officers feel that the material is not relevant to the prosecution case but may be useful to the defence in cross-examination, it may well come within the category of material which undermines the prosecution case. This is the test, not the fact that the evidence has been recorded; answer C is therefore incorrect.

In *Tucker* v *Crown Prosecution Service* [2008] EWCA Crim 3063, the prosecution never revealed to the defence the record containing important information as to a possible motive for a witness lying about the defendant's involvement in the offence, which led to the conviction being overturned. This was clearly material that undermined the prosecution case as it raised questions over the value of the witness's evidence. There does not need to be compelling evidence of this and the fact that there is other evidence supporting the prosecution case does not undermine this duty; answers A and B are therefore incorrect.

Evidence and Procedure, para. 2.5.6.4

Answer 5.2

Answer **B** — The Criminal Procedure and Investigations Act 1996 is primarily concerned with the disclosure of material which does not form part of the prosecution case resulting from a criminal investigation (i.e. 'unused material'). A criminal investigation is defined by s. 1(4) of the 1996 Act and para. 2.1(1)(a)–(c) of the Code of Practice. In order to satisfy the disclosure requirements, police officers should consider recording and retaining material in the early stages of an investigation. This will include:

• investigations into crimes that have been committed;
• investigations whose purpose is to ascertain whether a crime has been committed, with a view to the possible institution of criminal proceedings; and

- investigations which begin in the belief that a crime may be committed, for example when the police keep premises or individuals under observation for a period of time, with a view to the possible institution of criminal proceedings; answer C is therefore incorrect.

In these cases, the investigation may well have started some time before the defendant became a suspect; answer D is therefore incorrect. In such cases, all the material from the investigation/operation would have to be reviewed to see if it is relevant to the defence case. In cases where there is a surveillance operation or observation point, it may be that the details of the observation point and the surveillance techniques would not be revealed but it would be necessary to retain material generating from it; answer A is therefore incorrect.

Evidence and Procedure, para. 2.5.5

Answer 5.3

Answer **A** — Sensitive material is material which the disclosure officer believes it is not in the public interest to disclose. While the general principle that governs the 1996 Act and Art. 6 of the European Convention is that material should not be withheld from the defence, sensitive material is an exception to this. In *Van Mechelen v Netherlands* (1997) 25 EHRR 647, the court stated that in some cases it may be necessary to withhold certain evidence from the defence so as to preserve the fundamental rights of another individual or to safeguard an important public interest. It should be noted that the court did recognise that the entitlement of disclosure of relevant evidence was not an absolute right but could only be restricted as was strictly necessary (answer D is incorrect). In *R v Keane* [1994] 1 WLR 746, Lord Taylor CJ stated that:

> the judge should carry out a balancing exercise, having regard both to the weight of the public interest in non-disclosure and to the importance of the documents to the issues of interest, present and potential, to the defence, and if the disputed material might prove a defendant's innocence or avoid a miscarriage of justice, the balance came down resoundingly in favour of disclosure.

Decisions as to what should be withheld from the defence are a matter for the court and, where necessary, an application to withhold the material must be made to the court (*R v Ward* [1993] 1 WLR 619). The application of public interest immunity was considered by the House of Lords in *R v H* [2004] UKHL 3. In this case, the defendants were charged with conspiracy to supply a Class A drug following a covert police investigation, and sought disclosure of material held by the prosecution relating to the investigation. The prosecution resisted the disclosure on the grounds of public interest immunity. The court held that if the material did not weaken the prosecution case or strengthen the defence, there would be no requirement to disclose it. Only in truly borderline cases should the prosecution seek a judicial ruling on the disclosability of material in its hands. In considering any disclosure issue, the trial judge had constantly to bear in mind the overriding principle that derogation from the principle of full disclosure had always to be the minimum necessary to protect the public interest in question and must never imperil the overall fairness of the trial. Once material is considered to be sensitive, then it should be disclosed only if the public interest application fails (unless abandoning the case is considered more appropriate); before such action is taken, there must be consultation between the Crown Prosecution Service (Unit Head or above) and police (ACC or above); answers B and C are therefore incorrect.

Evidence and Procedure, para. 2.5.9.3

Answer 5.4

Answer **B** — In proceedings before the Crown Court, where the prosecutor has provided initial disclosure, or purported to, the accused must serve a defence statement on the prosecutor and the court. The accused must also provide details of any witnesses he/she intends to call at the trial; answers A, C and D are therefore incorrect.

Evidence and Procedure, para. 2.5.11.2

Answer 5.5

Answer **D** — The duty on the defence to make disclosure only arises after the prosecution has made the initial disclosure. The disclosure required by the defence is limited to material that it intends to use at trial.

The defence statement should set out the nature of the defendant's defence, including any particular defences on which he/she intends to rely and particulars of the matters of fact on which the defendant intends to rely; this means the defence will need to disclose a factual narrative of its case. The defence statement must indicate any point of law (including any point as to the admissibility of evidence or an abuse of process) which the defendant wishes to raise, and any authority on which he/she intends to rely for that purpose. Where the defence case involves an alibi, the statement must give details of the alibi, including the name and address of any alibi witness. The defence must also give to the court and the prosecutor notice of any witnesses other than the defendant who will be called to give evidence.

So it's all these facts that the defence statement must contain; answers A, B and C are therefore incorrect.

Evidence and Procedure, para. 2.5.11.1

Answer 5.6

Answer **D** — The duty is on the prosecution to continue to review the disclosure of prosecution material right up until the case is completed (acquittal, conviction or discontinuance of the case), and answer A is therefore incorrect. Material must be disclosed if the prosecutor forms the opinion that there is material which might undermine the prosecution case or might reasonably be expected to assist the accused's defence. Even if the information did not undermine the prosecution case, the material might have to be disclosed, and answer B is therefore incorrect. It is worth asking a number of pertinent questions: Would the previous statement bring the witness's credibility into question? Would this then assist the accused's defence? If the answer to both these questions is 'yes', the prosecutor would have to do more than just retain the information: it would have to be disclosed immediately to allow the defence an opportunity effectively to cross-examine the witness, and answer C is therefore incorrect.

Evidence and Procedure, para. 2.5.11.6

Answer 5.7

Answer **B** — In the Criminal Procedure and Investigations Act 1996 Code of Practice at para. 3.7 it is outlined that if, during a criminal investigation, the officer in charge of an investigation or disclosure officer for any reason no longer has responsibility for the functions falling to him/her, either his/her supervisor or the police officer in charge of investigations within the police force concerned must assign someone else to assume that responsibility. That person's identity must be recorded, as with those initially responsible for these functions in each investigation.

So it can be either the supervisor or the police officer in charge of criminal investigations for the police force concerned who has responsibility for reassigning the role, and there is no need to consult the Crown Prosecution Service on this matter; answers A, C and D are therefore incorrect.

Evidence and Procedure, para. 2.5.6

Answer 5.8

Answer **D** — Answers A and B are incorrect as para. 6.5 of the Disclosure Code of Practice states that irrespective of the anticipated plea, the common law test for disclosure requires material to be disclosed if there is material known to the disclosure officer that might assist the defence with the early preparation of its case or at a bail hearing (e.g. a key prosecution witness has relevant previous convictions or a witness has withdrawn his/her statement). A note must be made on the case summary for the prosecutor of any such material, which must be revealed to the prosecutor who will review it and consider whether it is disclosable (the prosecutor not the disclosure officer—so answer C is incorrect). Where there is no such material, a certificate to that effect must be completed.

Evidence and Procedure, para. 2.5.9

Answer 5.9

Answer **B** — Statements made by witnesses during an investigation of a complaint against a police officer are disclosable; however, the timing of the disclosure may be controlled—answer A is therefore incorrect. This is the case even if criminal charges are not raised; answer D is therefore incorrect.

In *R v Police Complaints Authority, ex parte Green* [2002] EWCA Civ 389, the Court of Appeal stated that there is no requirement to disclose witness statements to eye-witness complainants during the course of an investigation. The evidence of such complainants could be contaminated and, therefore, disclosure would risk hindering or frustrating the very purpose of the investigation. A complainant's legitimate interests were appropriately and adequately safeguarded by his/her right to a thorough and independent investigation, to contribute to the evidence, to be kept informed of the progress of the investigation and to be given reasoned conclusions on completion of the investigation. However, a complainant had no right to participate in the investigation as though he/she were supervising it. The general rule was that complainants, whether victims or next of kin, were not entitled to the disclosure of witness statements used in the course of a police investigation until its conclusion at the earliest. Note that disclosure can be made to next of kin; answer C is therefore incorrect.

Evidence and Procedure, para. 2.5.13.2

Answer 5.10

Answer **B** — This issue was examined in the case of *R* v *Lowe* [2003] EWCA Crim 3182. It was held in this case that there may be occasions where the defence statement is allowed to be used in cross-examination; namely, when it is alleged that the defendant has changed his/her defence or in re-examination to rebut a suggestion of recent invention. Answer A is therefore incorrect.

Such a request will not be granted on every occasion, therefore answer D is incorrect. There is no requirement for the defendant to be facing a charge of perjury, therefore answer C is incorrect.

Evidence and Procedure, para. 2.5.11.1

Answer 5.11

Answer **A** — Once the prosecution provides the initial disclosure, the defence has 14 days in respect of summary proceedings, or 28 days in respect of Crown Court proceedings, within which the accused in criminal proceedings must give a compulsory defence statement under s. 5 of the Act. Although this can be extended by the courts, there is no 'leeway' as such; answers B and C are therefore incorrect. However, the courts have held that even if the defence serves the defence statement outside the time limits the prosecution must still consider the impact of the statement in terms of the need for any further disclosure (*Murphy* v *DPP* [2006] EWHC 1753 (Admin)); answer D is therefore incorrect.

Evidence and Procedure, para. 2.5.11.5

Answer 5.12

Answer **D** — In *R* v *Johnson* [1988] 1 WLR 1377, Watkins LJ at pp. 1385–6 gave the following guidance as to the minimum evidential requirements needed if disclosure were to be protected:

> The police officer in charge of the observations, no one of a lower rank than a *sergeant* should usually be acceptable for this purpose, must be able to testify that beforehand he/ she visited all observation places to be used and ascertained the attitude of the occupiers of the premises, not only to their use, but the possible disclosure thereafter of the use which could lead to identification of the premises and the occupiers.

This makes answer D correct and answer B incorrect.

Prior to a trial, a police officer of no lower rank than a chief inspector must be able to testify that immediately prior to the trial he/she visited the places used for observations, the results of which it is proposed to give in evidence, and ascertained whether the occupiers were the same as when the observations took place and the attitude of the occupiers to possible disclosure of the use previously made of the premises (this makes answers A and C incorrect).

Evidence and Procedure, para. 2.5.9.5

6 | Detention and Treatment of Persons by Police Officers

Question 6.1

Inspector WILKINSON is on duty at a designated police station. There are no sergeants in the custody unit and no other sergeant in the police station is readily available.

In relation to who can perform custody duties in these circumstances, which of the following is correct?

A Only an officer of the rank of sergeant may perform the role of custody officer.

B Only an officer of the rank of sergeant may perform the role of custody officer or a constable if a sergeant is not readily available to perform the duties.

C Inspector WILKINSON can always perform the role of custody officer.

D Inspector WILKINSON can perform the role of custody officer if a sergeant is not readily available to perform the duties.

Question 6.2

HILL is in custody for a theft offence and has been searched. A number of items are to be retained by the custody officer and HILL is asked to sign the custody record that this is a true record of property. However, HILL refuses to sign the custody record.

Which of the following is correct in relation to Code C of PACE Codes of Practice?

A The custody officer need take no action as there is no requirement for HILL to sign for anything other than his rights.

B The custody officer should just note that HILL refused to sign the custody record.

C The custody officer should note that HILL refused to sign the custody record and the time he refused.

D The custody officer should note that HILL refused to sign the custody record, the time he refused and the reason given for that refusal.

Question 6.3

Constable PETROV has arrested ATKINS for criminal damage at the inquiry office of a non-designated police station, where she works alone. Constable PETROV intends dealing with ATKINS at her own station as he is likely to be in custody only for an hour. Constable PETROV has called for assistance from Constable FRY, who works in a neighbouring station.

Would it be appropriate for Constable PETROV to act as custody officer for ATKINS in these circumstances?

A Yes, provided she informs an on-duty inspector of her intention.

B No, she is the officer in the case and must await the arrival of Constable FRY, who should act as custody officer.

C Yes, provided she informs an inspector at a designated station of her intention.

D No, ATKINS may not be dealt with at a non-designated station.

Question 6.4

HIGGINS is in custody and requests his mother be informed of his arrest. He is later transferred to another police station as the one he was in had a fire and had to be closed. He requests that his girlfriend is informed of his new location.

In relation to this, which of the following is correct?

A He has already informed someone of his arrest and he has no right to have someone else informed.

B The person he informed initially must be informed that he has been moved to another police station.

C He can only have his mother informed that he has moved locations, but it will be his choice.

D At the new station, he is entitled again to have one person informed of his whereabouts.

Question 6.5

BAKER has been arrested for the theft of a mobile phone from a motor vehicle. BAKER was arrested near the vehicle and was alone. He asks that a friend of his be informed of his arrest and there is no answer. BAKER nominates another friend who also cannot be contacted. He then asks for his mother to be informed, she also does not answer. Finally, he asks if his brother can be informed.

In relation to this, which of the following is correct in regard to having someone informed of your whereabouts whilst in police custody?

A   BAKER can have his brother informed at the custody officer's discretion.

B   The custody officer must inform BAKER's brother as PACE requires him to do so.

C   The custody officer need not inform the brother as he has made at least two attempts to contact someone.

D   The custody officer need not inform the brother as he has made at least three attempts to contact someone.

Question 6.6

MARSHALL has been arrested for murder and arrived at the designated police station at 8 am; his detention was authorised at 8.15 am. Police exercised the right to hold the suspect incommunicado at 9 am. MARSHALL became ill and was taken to hospital where he remained for five hours. During this time he was not questioned about the offence.

By what time, assuming the maximum time allowed is used, will the right to hold the suspect incommunicado end?

A   8 pm the following day, 36 hours after arrival at the police station.

B   8.15 pm the following day, 36 hours after detention was authorised.

C   9 pm the following day, 36 hours after the decision to exercise the right.

D   1 pm the following day, 36 hours after arrival at the police station taking out the five hours not in detention at the hospital.

Question 6.7

O'REILLY has been arrested for armed robbery of a building society, where £50,000 was stolen. The officer in the case has proposed that O'REILLY be denied his right to have someone informed of his arrest, as it may alert his accomplice who has not yet been arrested. The duty inspector is engaged at a firearms incident but she can be contacted by mobile phone.

Would it be lawful for the inspector to authorise a delay to O'REILLY's rights over the telephone in these circumstances?

A Yes, but the decision must be recorded in writing within 24 hours.

B No, the authorisation must be given by an officer not below the rank of superintendent.

C Yes, but the decision must be recorded in writing as soon as practicable.

D No, the authorisation must be made in person.

Question 6.8

DAWLISH has been arrested for robbery and has indicated that he wishes to have legal advice. There is a significant delay in his solicitor attending and he indicated that he would be willing to be interviewed without the solicitor. During the interview, his solicitor arrives and the interviewing officer is informed; the interviewing officer has indicated that if the suspect sees his solicitor immediately another suspect may be tipped off. He asks to carry on the interview without a solicitor until the other suspect is identified by DAWLISH.

In these circumstances, which of the following is correct?

A In these circumstances, the suspect must be allowed to consult with his solicitor immediately; there are no exceptions.

B In these circumstances, the interview can continue and the suspect can then be informed that his solicitor has arrived as he stated that he did not require one.

C The consultation with the solicitor can be delayed provided an officer of the rank of inspector or above authorises it.

D The consultation with the solicitor can be delayed provided an officer of the rank of superintendent or above authorises it.

Question 6.9

PRINCE was arrested at 10 am in Reading (Thames Valley Police area) for an offence of theft. PRINCE arrived at the police station at 10.15 am, when it was discovered that she was wanted for an offence of theft in Bristol (Avon and Somerset Police area). PRINCE was interviewed and charged with theft, and at 3 pm the same day she was taken to Bristol to be interviewed, arriving at the custody office at Bristol Police Station at 4.30 pm.

What would PRINCE's 'relevant time' be in relation to her detention in Bristol?

A 10 am.

B 3 pm.

C 10.15 am.

D 4.30 pm.

Question 6.10

Inspector WISLICKI is carrying out a review of the detention of a male arrested for a violence offence. The inspector asks if there are any representations the detainee wishes to make about his detention and the detainee starts shouting and swearing at the inspector.

In relation to this, which of the following is correct?

A Inspector WISLICKI must listen to the representations unless the detainee is drunk.

B Inspector WISLICKI should listen to the representations even if they are abusive.

C Inspector WISLICKI may refuse to listen to representations from the detainee if the officer considers them unfit to make representations because of their condition or behaviour.

D Inspector WISLICKI may refuse to listen to representations from the detainee if the officer considers them unfit to make representations because of their condition or behaviour but then must take representations from the detainee's legal adviser.

Question 6.11

JACKSON has been arrested for affray and assault on police. On arrival at the custody suite, JACKSON is extremely violent; shouting, screaming, intoxicated and attempting to bite any officers or Designated Detention Officers. As such, he is immediately placed straight into a cell via a controlled cell entry and exit. PACE Code C gives guidance as to what a custody officer must record on a custody record when detaining a person with or without charge.

What details should be recorded on the custody record in these circumstances?

A The grounds for detention in the person's presence, unless it is apparent that he would not understand what was being said.

B The grounds for detention in the person's presence, regardless of his condition.

C The grounds for the person's detention which can be recorded at any time whilst in custody.

D The grounds for detention in the person's presence, if it is practicable to do so.

Question 6.12

BROWN, MORSE and ROBERTS have been arrested for criminal damage to a shop window. A witness saw one person from the group throwing a stone through the window, but was not able to identify the exact person who caused the damage. BROWN has been interviewed by Constable KEANE, and the officer has asked the custody officer for him to be detained until the other two suspects are interviewed.

Under what circumstances may the custody officer detain BROWN further in these circumstances?

A BROWN may be detained if the custody officer has reasonable grounds to believe it is necessary to preserve evidence.

B BROWN should be released as there is insufficient evidence against him to secure a conviction.

C BROWN may be detained if the custody officer has reasonable cause to suspect it is necessary to preserve evidence.

D BROWN must be detained until the investigation is complete against all three defendants.

Question 6.13

Constable DEAR has attended at a large department store to deal with a person suspected of theft. The officer arrests the person at 3.15 pm and decides to release them on street bail in accordance with s. 30 of the Police and Criminal Evidence Act 1984. The person is bailed at 3.30 pm to attend at police station 'A' at 6 pm. Unfortunately, the person misunderstands the instructions and arrives at police station 'B' which is nearer their home; they arrive at 6 pm. They are redirected to police station 'A' arriving at that police station front counter at 6.45 pm in accordance with their bail. They are taken through to the custody unit and detention is authorised at 7.20 pm.

What is the 'relevant time' as outlined in the Police and Criminal Evidence Act 1984?

A 3.30 pm, the time they were bailed.

B 6 pm, the time of arrival at the first police station in that force area.

C 6.45 pm, the time of arrival at the police station to which the notice of bail states they must attend.

D 7.20 pm, the time their detention is authorised.

Question 6.14

STIRLING has been arrested for a summary offence. At 10 pm, DC MUTKI approached the custody officer, stating that he was not in a position to charge STIRLING and that a vital witness had been identified who would not be available until 9 am the following day. DC MUTKI asked if a superintendent could authorise STIRLING's continued detention beyond 24 hours in order to speak to the witness. STIRLING has been in custody for 14 hours.

Could a superintendent authorise such a request at this stage of STIRLING's detention?

A Yes, but only after he has been in custody for at least 15 hours.

B No, not until he has been in custody for 24 hours.

C Yes, but only after an inspector has conducted a second review.

D No, as STIRLING has not been arrested for an indictable offence.

Question 6.15

CLYDE has been arrested on suspicion of rape. His detention has been extended by the superintendent for up to 36 hours without charge. Under ss. 43 and 44 of the Police and Criminal Evidence Act 1984, where a person has been in custody for 36 hours without being charged, the police must apply to a magistrate to extend that person's detention beyond that time.

What is the total amount of detention time that can be authorised by magistrates beyond the original 36 hours before a person must be charged or released? (Do not consider offences under the Terrorism Act 2000.)

A 24 hours.

B 36 hours.

C 48 hours.

D 60 hours.

Question 6.16

ADAMS is in custody for an offence of burglary and has requested legal advice. The legal representative who attends is from a firm which has persistently sent probationary representatives who are unsuited to proving the appropriate legal advice. The custody inspector is seeking to escalate his concerns.

Which of the following is correct in relation to this process of escalation:

A The inspector should inform an officer of at least superintendent rank, who may wish to take the matter up with the Solicitors Regulation Authority.

B The inspector should inform an officer of at least chief inspector rank, who may wish to take the matter up with the Solicitors Regulation Authority.

C The inspector should inform an officer of at least superintendent rank, who must take the matter up with the Solicitors Regulation Authority.

D The inspector should inform an officer of at least chief inspector rank, who must take the matter up with the Solicitors Regulation Authority.

Question 6.17

CROCKER was charged and acquitted of a charge of murder by the Crown Court. Following further inquiries, he was arrested under the Criminal Justice Act 2003 for that same murder and is in custody at the police station; CROCKER is not precluded from further prosecution by the Court of Appeal.

Who is responsible for determining whether there is sufficient evidence to charge CROCKER with murder again?

A The custody officer.

B An officer of the rank of superintendent or above who has not been directly involved in the investigation.

C An officer of at least the rank of assistant chief constable (commander in the Metropolitan Police).

D The Director of Public Prosecutions (DPP).

Question 6.18

DE LACY has been arrested for an indictable only offence (the relevant time is 11 pm on Monday) and is in custody at the city centre police station. The superintendent of that police station will be on leave from 1 pm on Tuesday and after that time there will be a rota outlining who the force 'on call' superintendent will be. DE LACY's detention clock will terminate at 11 pm on Tuesday and the officer in charge of the investigation considers that an extension of the detention clock is required; the second review is due at 2 pm on Tuesday.

What must the officer in charge of the investigation do to ensure an extension is granted?

A The superintendent responsible for the city centre police station must authorise the extension prior to terminating duty.

B The superintendent responsible for the city centre police station must authorise the extension prior to terminating duty, so the second review will have to be brought forward.

C The on-call superintendent can authorise the extension at any time up to 11 pm on Tuesday.

D The on-call superintendent can authorise the extension up to 11 pm on Tuesday but only after the second review.

Question 6.19

THRUSH was arrested on warrant for failing to answer bail to appear at court and is in police custody awaiting court in the morning.

Which of the following is correct in relation to reviews of this detention?

A His detention should be reviewed by an inspector, timings as statutory reviews.

B His detention should be reviewed by the custody officer, timings as statutory reviews.

C His detention should be reviewed by an inspector, periodically.

D His detention should be reviewed by the custody officer, periodically.

Question 6.20

KEY was arrested for affray, and on his arrival at the custody suite he was violent towards the custody officer. KEY was taken to a cell because of his behaviour and, because he had not been searched, the custody officer ordered him to be searched in the cell. The arresting officer, who was female, was present in the cell when KEY was searched by the male custody staff.

Have the provisions of s. 54 of the Police and Criminal Evidence Act 1984 (searching of detained persons) been complied with in these circumstances?

A Yes, a female officer may search a male prisoner, provided it is not an intimate search.

B Yes, provided the female officer did not conduct the search.

C No, the female officer should not have been present at the search.

D Yes, a female officer may search a male prisoner, provided it is not a strip search.

Question 6.21

MURTAGH was arrested and interviewed in relation to a terrorist offence and there is sufficient evidence to charge him. During the interviews, MURTAGH was denied access to a solicitor and the charging officer is considering how MURTAGH should be cautioned when charged.

What should the words of this caution be?

A You do not have to say anything. But it may harm your defence if you do not mention now something which you later rely on in court. Anything you do say may be given in evidence.

B You do not have to say anything. But it may harm your defence if you do not mention when questioned something which you later rely on in court. Anything you do say may be given in evidence.

C You do not have to say anything, but anything you do say may be given in evidence.

D You do not have to say anything, but anything you do say will be noted down, and may be given in evidence.

Question 6.22

KENWRIGHT was arrested and taken to the custody office of a designated police station. The arresting officer told the custody officer that KENWRIGHT had a warning signal on the Police National Computer (PNC) that, while in custody previously, she had concealed razor blades in her mouth and had used them to cause injury to herself. The custody officer decided that KENWRIGHT's mouth should be searched for objects which she might use to harm herself.

Which of the following is true in relation to the search?

A The custody officer can authorise this search at the custody office.

B Only a superintendent can authorise this search at the custody office.

C An inspector can authorise this search at medical premises.

D Only a superintendent can authorise this search at medical premises.

Question 6.23

STAINES has been in custody since 07:30 hours and the time is now 15:30. According to the custody record, during this time he has received several hot drinks, an all-day breakfast and a hot lunch but is demanding that he has not been fed sufficiently and that meals are being withheld from him. In relation to the treatment and welfare of a detained person, PACE Code C, para. 8.6 describes how many meals a detainee should be offered while in custody.

How many meals should be offered to a detained person in any period of 24 hours?

A At least one light meal and at least two main meals.
B At least one light meal and at least one main meal.
C At least two light meals and at least one main meal.
D At least two light meals and at least two main meals.

Question 6.24

GORTAT has been arrested on suspicion of handling stolen goods and has been presented to the custody sergeant who has authorised his detention. ALLPRESS is employed as a detention officer by his local police authority and has been instructed by the custody sergeant to take non-intimate samples, fingerprints and photographs from GORTAT. ALLPRESS is new and is unsure whether he can perform all, or any, of these instructions.

In relation to duties that he can perform, which of the following is correct?

A He may take a non-intimate sample but he may not use force to do so.
B He may take a non-intimate sample and may use force to do so where necessary.
C He may take fingerprints and photographs but may not take non-intimate samples.
D He may take photographs but may not take fingerprints or non-intimate samples.

Question 6.25

HURTY was stopped while driving his vehicle on a Saturday morning in Margate (Kent Police area). The officer who stopped him, Constable DICKINSON, conducted a Police National Computer (PNC) check and discovered that HURTY was wanted for an offence of burglary in Newcastle (Northumbria Police area). Constable DICKINSON arrested HURTY at 10 am and took him to the nearest designated station (Margate Police Station), where they arrived at 10.30 am. Constable DICKINSON contacted the police in Newcastle; however, they had no officers available to attend until later that day. The escorting officers finally arrived in the early hours of the next morning, and left with HURTY at 4 am on the Sunday. They transported HURTY to Newcastle, arriving in that force area at 11.10 am; they eventually arrived at Newcastle Police Station at 11.30 am on the Sunday.

What would HURTY's 'relevant time' be in relation to his detention in Newcastle?
A 10.30 am on the Saturday.
B 10 am on the Sunday.
C 11.10 am on the Sunday.
D 11.30 am on the Sunday.

Question 6.26

Constable MOLE arrested WOOD at 3 pm on a Saturday for an offence of theft. Constable MOLE radioed through to her station but discovered that the custody office could not accept her prisoner at that time as they were too busy. She decided to utilise her powers under s. 30A of the Police and Criminal Evidence Act 1984 to bail WOOD to the police station the next day. WOOD was released on bail by the officer at 3.30 pm on the Saturday. WOOD was due to answer bail at 2 pm on the Sunday but he was late and arrived there at 2.30 pm. His detention was authorised by the custody officer at 2.50 pm.

From which time on the Sunday would WOOD's 'relevant time' be calculated, under s. 41 of the Police and Criminal Evidence Act 1984?
A 2.50 pm, the time he appeared before the custody officer on the Sunday.
B 2.20 pm, taking into account the time he was detained by the officer the previous day.
C 2.30 pm, the time he arrived at the police station on the Sunday.
D 2 pm, the time he was due to answer bail on the Sunday.

Question 6.27

MORRISON was arrested for shoplifting and taken to the custody office. On MORRISON's arrival, the custody officer noticed that he was intoxicated. MORRISON was detained for interview and placed in a cell to allow him time to sober up. While he was asleep, MORRISON's sister contacted the custody officer to advise that MORRISON was an alcoholic and might get the shakes while in custody. When he was sober, MORRISON was interviewed and returned to his cell pending preparation of charges. He displayed no symptoms of the shakes and did not complain of an illness. Unfortunately, while he was in his cell, MORRISON died from asphyxiation. MORRISON was not medically examined while in custody.

Would the police have any liability in relation to the custody officer's failure to act on the information given by MORRISON's sister, and not arranging for him to be medically examined?

A No, as MORRISON's sister is not a registered health care professional or doctor.

B Yes, a custody officer should act on any information relating to a detainee's health care, no matter what the source.

C No, since MORRISON displayed no symptoms of his illness and did not ask to see a doctor.

D Yes, but only if MORRISON's sister informed the custody officer that he was taking medication or seeking medical help for his condition.

Question 6.28

Student Police Officer MILES has made his first arrest and is waiting in the police vehicle in the yard of the police station with his detained person and his tutor—PC ROWLINGS—as the custody suite is extremely busy. Whilst waiting, PC ROWLINGS tells PC MILES that Code C, para. 2.1A of the PACE Codes of Practice defines when a detained person will be deemed to be 'at a police station' for the purposes of detention. He asks PC MILES when would they be deemed as 'at a police station' with their detained person.

Which of the following statements would be the correct response from PC MILES according to the Codes of Practice?

A When the person first arrives within the confines of the custody office, whether or not the custody officer is ready to receive them.

B When the person is first brought before the custody officer, within the confines of the custody office.

C When the person first arrives inside a police station, whether this is the custody office or another part of the building.

D When the person first arrives within the confines of the police station, whether this is inside the building or in an enclosed yard which is part of the police station.

Question 6.29

BRAITHWAITE is 13 years of age and was arrested for an offence of aggravated vehicle-taking. On his arrival at the custody office, BRAITHWAITE declined legal advice and stated that neither of his parents would attend the police station to act as an appropriate adult. BOYCE works for the local Youth Offending Team (YOT) and attended to act as appropriate adult. On arrival at the custody office, BOYCE told the custody officer that it was their policy that all juveniles represented by the YOT must also be represented by a solicitor. BOYCE insisted on a solicitor being called.

Would BOYCE be able to overrule BRAITHWAITE's decision and ensure that he seeks legal advice?

A Yes, as BOYCE was acting in BRAITHWAITE's best interests.

B No, BOYCE had no right to ask for a solicitor to attend once BRAITHWAITE had declined legal advice.

C Yes, because BRAITHWAITE is under 14 and it is in his best interests.

D No, the decision remains with BRAITHWAITE, who does not have to speak to the solicitor.

Question 6.30

PC O'HARA has detained PIGGOTT in order to conduct a s. 1 PACE stop and search of him. During the search, PC O'HARA located a lock-knife and subsequently arrested PIGGOTT and conveyed him to custody. On arrival, PC O'HARA informed the custody sergeant of the grounds for the arrest but PIGGOTT maintained that the officer was lying and that he had planted the knife.

According to Code C, para. 3.4 of the PACE Codes of Practice, which of the following statements is correct in relation to the comments made by PIGGOTT?

A The PACE Codes state that the custody officer shall note on the custody record any comment the detainee makes in relation to the arresting officer's account and shall invite comment.

B The PACE Codes state that the custody officer shall note on the custody record any comment the detainee makes in relation to the arresting officer's account but shall not invite comment.

C The PACE Codes state that the custody officer may use discretion as to whether he/she shall note on the custody record any comment the detainee makes in relation to the arresting officer's account.

D The PACE Codes state that the custody officer is not required to note on the custody record any comment the detainee makes in relation to the arresting officer's account.

Question 6.31

BLAKE has been detained, without charge, on suspicion of aggravated burglary.

What is the maximum period BLAKE may be detained for?
A 96 hours.
B 7 days.
C 14 days.
D 28 days.

Question 6.32

CLYDE has been arrested for an offence of kidnapping and the relevant time began at 10 am on Tuesday. Unfortunately, he became ill and had to go to hospital; he left the custody unit at 4 pm arriving at the hospital at 4.30 pm. He remained at the hospital until 9.30 pm and arrived back in custody at 10 pm. Throughout his time in hospital, officers remained with him hoping to interview him regarding the whereabouts of the yet unfound victim. However, the casualty doctors refused to allow any questioning of CLYDE.

At what time will CLYDE's detention time end (assuming no extensions are applied for or granted)?
A 10 am on Wednesday; the hospital time counts as officers were present intending to interview CLYDE.
B 3 pm on Wednesday; standard detention time excluding the time spent in hospital.
C 3.30 pm on Wednesday; standard detention time excluding the time spent in hospital and travelling to hospital.
D 4 pm on Wednesday; standard detention time excluding the time spent in hospital and time travelling to and from hospital.

Question 6.33

NORMAN is in custody for an offence. She requested legal advice and was allowed to consult on the telephone with the duty solicitor. Shortly afterwards, another solicitor, GULLIVER, summoned by NORMAN's father, attended at the police station.

In relation to GULLIVER, which of the following is correct?

A GULLIVER must be allowed a private consultation with NORMAN.

B NORMAN does not need to be told about GULLIVER as she has already received legal advice.

C NORMAN must be told that GULLIVER is present and should be allowed a consultation.

D NORMAN does not need to be told about GULLIVER as she did not request advice from him.

Question 6.34

A suspect fell from a roof during a burglary and was arrested but had to be taken to hospital. The officers fear for the safety of another person still missing and wish to interview the suspect.

In relation to this, which of the following is correct?

A They cannot interview the suspect while he is a patient in hospital.

B They can interview the suspect with the agreement of a responsible doctor.

C They can interview the suspect only with the agreement of the doctor in charge of the suspect's care and the authority of an officer of the rank of inspector or above.

D They can interview the suspect with the agreement of the doctor in charge of the suspect's care and the custody officer at the nearest designated station.

Question 6.35

Code C, para. 13.4 gives guidance in relation to written statements under caution from suspects, when the statement is made in a language other than English and an interpreter is present.

What does this Code of Practice state in relation to who should write the statement under caution?

A The interpreter should record the statement in the language in which it is made, the person shall be invited to sign it and an official English translation shall be made there and then.

B The interviewee should record it in his/her own language, sign it and the interpreter should translate it there and then.

C The interpreter should record the statement in the language in which it is made, the person shall be invited to sign it and an official English translation shall be made in due course.

D The interviewee should record it in his/her own language, sign it and the interpreter should translate it in due course.

Question 6.36

O'SULLIVAN was in detention, having been arrested for burglary. Two people escaped from the police at the scene with the stolen property. When O'SULLIVAN's detention was first authorised, he declined legal advice. Constable GOODE, the investigating officer, wished to interview O'SULLIVAN straight away because of the outstanding property and to establish who had been with O'SULLIVAN. However, it was discovered that O'SULLIVAN had injured his leg and the custody officer determined that he had to go to hospital after detention was authorised. The custody officer agreed that Constable GOODE could accompany O'SULLIVAN to hospital and interview him there. It transpired that O'SULLIVAN was cooperative and the officer asked him some questions in the ambulance and further questions at the hospital with permission from a doctor.

Assuming that Constable GOODE followed the Codes of Practice relating to cautioning suspects and legal advice prior to the interviews, how much time will count towards O'SULLIVAN's overall detention time when he returns to the custody office?

A The whole time spent away from the custody office.

B The whole time spent at the hospital.

C Only the time spent during the interview at the hospital.

D Only the time spent questioning him.

Question 6.37

In certain circumstances, Code C, para. 6.9 of the PACE Codes of Practice allows the removal of a legal representative from an interview because of their behaviour.

Which of the following statements is correct in relation to the authorisation required to implement para. 6.9?

A A superintendent may make such an authorisation but, if one is not available, it may be done by an inspector.

B Only an inspector or above may make such an authorisation.

C Either a superintendent or an inspector or above may make an authorisation, but only if they witness the behaviour.

D Only a superintendent or above may make such an authorisation.

Question 6.38

CALLARD has been arrested and is about to be interviewed on audio. Initially, CALLARD stated that he did not want a solicitor and the interview commenced. As the officer commences the interview and reminds him of his right to legal advice, CALLARD indicates that he would like legal advice and asks what will happen. The officer says the interview will stop and a solicitor will be called. CALLARD indicates that he does not want to go back in a cell and says he wants to be interviewed now and not wait and does not want a solicitor.

In the circumstances outlined in the scenario, can the audio-recorded interview proceed?

A Yes, provided an officer of the rank of inspector or above has given agreement for the interview to proceed in these circumstances.

B Yes, provided an officer of the rank of inspector has given agreement and the suspect agrees in writing.

C No, as CALLARD has stated that he has changed his mind over legal advice during the interview his solicitor must be contacted.

D No, CALLARD changed his mind due to what the officer said, in these circumstances a solicitor must be called.

Question 6.39

KRIEGER (a juvenile) has been arrested for an offence of assault and taken to a designated police station. The custody officer, PS WILSHER, opens a custody record in respect of KRIEGER and contacts KRIEGER's mother to act as an appropriate adult. Thirty minutes later, KRIEGER's mother arrives at the station and is shown into the custody block. Mrs KRIEGER is informed of the circumstances of the arrest and, in the presence of his mother, KRIEGER is given his rights again (having been given them initially on arrival at the station). KRIEGER asks for a solicitor and his mother agrees with her son. At this point, Mrs KRIEGER states 'I know a bit about the law myself, so I'd like to have a look at my son's custody record, please.'

Which of the following statements is correct with regard to Mrs KRIEGER's entitlement to examine her son's custody record?

A Other than police officers, the only person permitted to examine KRIEGER's custody record would be his solicitor.

B If an officer of the rank of inspector or above authorises it, Mrs KRIEGER can consult her son's custody record.

C Mrs KRIEGER can examine her son's custody record when she initially arrives at the station, but will not be permitted to do so at any other time.

D Mrs KRIEGER must be permitted to consult her son's custody record as soon as is practicable and at any other time whilst her son is detained.

Question 6.40

EVANS has been arrested on suspicion of unlawful possession of a controlled substance (Class A drugs) and has been taken to custody. On arrival, the custody sergeant has authorised that EVANS be searched and two male officers begin to do so. Having been 'asked' to remove his trousers and underwear, he is then 'asked to separate his penis and testicles, to pull his foreskin back and then to turn around and lean over, separating his bottom cheeks'. This was to check whether Class A drugs had been secreted in these areas.

With regards to PACE Code C, does this amount to an intimate search?

A Yes, as the physical examination of a person's body orifices other than the mouth defines an intimate search.

B Yes, although this would be unlawful as this has not been authorised by an officer of inspector rank.

C No, because EVANS was 'asked' to do so and this is therefore classified as a search with consent.

D No, because the examination taking place is visual only with no penetrative exploration inside the body.

ANSWERS

Answer 6.1

Answer **D** — Section 36 of the Police and Criminal Evidence Act 1984 requires that one or more custody officers must be appointed for each designated police station. However, in *Vince* v *Chief Constable of Dorset* [1993] 1 WLR 415, it was held that a chief constable was under a duty to appoint one custody officer for each designated police station and had a discretionary power to appoint more than one but this duty did not go so far as to require a sufficient number to ensure that the functions of custody officer were always performed by them.

The provision of the facility of a custody officer must be reasonable. Section 36(3) states that a custody officer must be an officer of at least the rank of sergeant. However, s. 36(4) allows officers of *any* rank to perform the functions of custody officer at a designated police station if a sergeant is not readily available to perform; answer A is therefore incorrect. This means that officers higher in rank than a sergeant can perform custody duties and not just constables; answer B is therefore incorrect. However, this is only where a sergeant is not readily available to perform the duties; answer C is therefore incorrect.

The effect of s. 36(3) and (4) is that the practice of allowing officers of any other rank to perform the role of custody officer where a sergeant (who has no other role to perform) is in the police station must therefore be unlawful.

Evidence and Procedure, para. 2.6.2

Answer 6.2

Answer **C** — Code C, para. 2.7 states:

> The fact and time of any detainee's refusal to sign a custody record, when asked in accordance with this Code, must be recorded.

There is nothing mentioned about a reason for that refusal; answers A, B and D are therefore incorrect.

Evidence and Procedure, para. 2.6.7

Answer 6.3

Answer **C** — Section 30 of the Police and Criminal Evidence Act 1984 requires that a person who has been arrested at a place other than a police station must be taken to a police station *as soon as practicable* after arrest, unless the arrested person has been released prior to arrival at the police station. Section 30A of the Act allows a constable to release on bail a person who is under arrest ('street bail'). However, an arrested person may be dealt with at a non-designated station, provided the person is not likely to be detained for longer than six hours. Answer D is therefore incorrect.

Where a person is taken to a non-designated station, s. 36(7) states that an officer of any rank not involved in the investigation should perform the role of custody officer. However, if no such person is at the station, the arresting officer (or any other officer involved in the investigation) may act as custody officer. Answer B is therefore incorrect.

Where a person is dealt with in a non-designated station in the circumstances described, an officer of at least the rank of inspector at a *designated station* must be informed. Answer A is therefore incorrect.

Evidence and Procedure, paras 2.6.4, 2.6.8

Answer 6.4

Answer **D** — A person in police detention is entitled to have one friend or relative or person known to him/her or who is likely to take an interest in his/her welfare informed of his/her whereabouts as soon as practicable (PACE Code C, para. 5.1); answer C is therefore incorrect.

Code C, paras 3.1 and 5.3 outline that this is a continuing right that applies every time a person is brought to a police station under arrest. The right may be exercised each time a detainee is taken to another police station.

This means that a person may have another person (or the same person) informed of his/her detention at the second station; answer A is therefore incorrect. Note it is the detained person's right; no one has the right to be told of detention without the detained person's permission; answer B is therefore incorrect.

Evidence and Procedure, paras 2.6.8, 2.6.10

Answer 6.5

Answer **A** — Any person arrested and held in custody at a police station or other premises may, on request, have one person known to them or likely to take an interest in his/her welfare informed at public expense of his/her whereabouts as soon as practicable. If the person cannot be contacted, the detainee may choose up to two alternatives. If they cannot be contacted, the person in charge of detention or the investigation has discretion to allow further attempts until the information has been conveyed.

So, on the fourth alternative contact it is at the discretion of the custody officer not mandated; answer B is therefore incorrect.

There are two alternatives, not three, but the custody officer can allow as many as they like; answers C and D are therefore incorrect.

Evidence and Procedure, para. 2.6.10

Answer 6.6

Answer **A** — Section 56 of the Police and Criminal Evidence Act 1984 provides that a person arrested and held in custody at a police station or other premises may, on request, have one friend or relative or person known to him/her or who is likely to take an interest in his/her welfare, informed at public expense of his/her where-abouts as soon as practicable (PACE Code C, para. 5.1). This right can only be de-layed if the offence is 'an indictable offence' and an officer of the rank of inspector or above (whether or not connected to the investigation) authorises the delay. The delay can only be for a maximum of 36 hours and this period is calculated from the 'relevant time'; that is, the time of arrival at the police station, i.e. 8 am. Note that this is not the time detention is authorised or the decision made to hold the sus-pect incommunicado; answers B and C are therefore incorrect. Although time spent in hospital does not count towards detention time, this does not affect the time a person can be held incommunicado which remains at 36 hours from the relevant time; answer D is therefore incorrect.

Evidence and Procedure, paras 2.6.10, 2.6.21

Answer 6.7

Answer **C** — First, the inspector must be satisfied that O'REILLY is in custody for an indictable offence (which is the case in the scenario). Also, the inspector must have reasonable grounds for believing that if O'REILLY were to exercise his right to have someone informed of his arrest, it might alert other people suspected of the offence but not yet arrested.

PACE Code C, Annex B states that the grounds for action under this Annex shall be recorded and the person informed of them as soon as practicable. The author-isation can initially be made orally, either in person or by telephone, but must be recorded in writing as soon as practicable. Answer D is therefore incorrect.

The decision must be recorded in writing *as soon as practicable*; therefore, answer A is incorrect.

The authorising officer for delaying rights under Code C, para. 5 was reduced from superintendent to inspector by virtue of s. 74 of the Criminal Justice and Police Act 2001; therefore, answer B is incorrect.

Evidence and Procedure, paras 2.6.10, 2.6.21

Answer 6.8

Answer **D** — It is acceptable for a suspect to change his/her mind about not having a solicitor present during an interview but, if one arrives whilst the suspect is being interviewed, the relevant legislation is applied again and the suspect must be told immediately (Code C, para. 6.15). As this must be done immediately, answer B is therefore incorrect.

The only exception to this is where Annex B of Code C applies and this right can be delayed for certain reasons; one of those reasons is that other people suspected of having committed an offence but not yet arrested for it could be alerted; answer A is therefore incorrect.

The initial change of mind about the right would be authorised by an inspector, but any delay in the right once the solicitor arrives must be authorised by a superintendent; answer C is therefore incorrect.

Evidence and Procedure, para. 2.6.11

Answer 6.9

Answer **D** — Under s. 41(2) of the Police and Criminal Evidence Act 1984, a person's 'relevant time' is calculated from the time he/she arrives at the police station, or 24 hours after he/she was arrested, whichever is earlier. Since most detainees arrive at the station well within 24 hours, their relevant time is generally when they first arrive at the station.

There are several variations contained within s. 41 of the 1984 Act, and the circumstances covered in the question are to be found in s. 41(5). Section 41 states:

(5) If—
  (a) a person is in police detention in a police area in England and Wales ('the first area'); and
  (b) his arrest for an offence is sought in some other police area in England and Wales ('the second area'); and

    (c) he is taken to the second area for the purposes of investigating that offence, without being questioned in the first area in order to obtain evidence in relation to it,

    the relevant time shall be—

        (i) the time 24 hours after he leaves the place where he is detained in the first area; *or*

        (ii) the time at which he arrives at the first police station to which he is taken in the second area,

    whichever is the earlier.

Note that under s. 41(5) the detainee has, in effect, two detention clocks running. It is important to note that the second clock will start earlier if the detained person is questioned about the offence under investigation in the other police area. However, in the scenario PRINCE was *not* questioned about the offence in the first station, and she arrived at the second station *less than 24 hours* after her departure from the first station. Her relevant time is, therefore, her time of arrival at the second station (i.e. 4.30 pm). Answers A, B and C are therefore incorrect.

Evidence and Procedure, para. 2.6.17.1

Answer 6.10

Answer **C** — Under PACE Code C (paras 15.3 to 15.3B), before deciding whether to authorise continued detention the officer responsible for the review shall give an opportunity to make representations about the detention to:

(a) the detainee, unless in the case of a review the detainee is asleep;

(b) the detainee's solicitor if available at the time; and

(c) the appropriate adult if available at the time.

Other people having an interest in the detainee's welfare may also make representations at the authorising officer's discretion.

    The representations may be made orally in person or by telephone or in writing. The authorising officer may, however, refuse to hear oral representations from the detainee if the officer considers them unfit to make representations because of their condition or behaviour; answers A and B are therefore incorrect.

    Should this happen, there is no need to ensure another person makes representations; answer D is therefore incorrect.

Evidence and Procedure, para. 2.6.18

Answer 6.11

Answer **D** — Under PACE Code C, para. 3.20B, a custody officer should record the grounds for detention in the person's presence if it is practicable to do so. Therefore, in cases such as when a person is drunk or violent, it may not be practicable to record the grounds in his/her presence. Answer B is therefore incorrect. This recording of the grounds must, by virtue of Code C, para. 3.4, be before that person is questioned about any offence; answer C is therefore incorrect.

Answer A is incorrect because if a person cannot understand what is being said, it may be 'impracticable' to record the grounds for detention in his/her presence; however, it is not written as such in the Codes of Practice.

Evidence and Procedure, paras 2.6.7, 2.6.8

Answer 6.12

Answer **A** — If the custody officer has determined that there is insufficient evidence to charge, the person must be released unless the custody officer has *reasonable grounds for believing* that the person's detention is necessary to preserve or to obtain evidence by questioning the person (s. 37 of the Police and Criminal Evidence Act 1984). Answer C is incorrect as 'reasonable grounds for believing' requires a greater amount of evidence than 'reasonable cause to suspect'.

Although the person may ultimately be detained until all the suspects are interviewed in these circumstances, each case must be considered on its own merit, against the previous criteria. Answer D is therefore incorrect.

Where the suspicion rests with several suspects, it may be appropriate to hold all suspects until they are all interviewed before deciding whether there is sufficient evidence to warrant a charge against any or all of them. This continues provided suspicion on that individual has not been dispelled in the interim and the questioning is not unnecessarily delayed (*Clarke* v *Chief Constable of North Wales* [2000] All ER (D) 477); answer B is therefore incorrect.

Evidence and Procedure, para. 2.6.8

Answer 6.13

Answer **C** — The 'relevant time' is worked out according to the relevant circumstances. Where a person is arrested and bailed at a place other than a police station, the time of arrival at the police station to which the notice of bail states he/she must attend is the relevant time. In this particular case, then, the relevant time is 6.45 pm and no account is taken of the time they are bailed or the time they arrived at the wrong police station (irrespective of the fact that it is in the same police area); answers A and B are therefore incorrect.

The time of detention relates to the review clock not the 'relevant time'; answer D is therefore incorrect.

Evidence and Procedure, para. 2.6.17.1

Answer 6.14

Answer **D** — An officer of at least the rank of superintendent can authorise a person's continued detention, beyond 24 hours, up to a maximum of 36 hours. The period can be shorter, but if a shorter period is granted, this can be extended up to the 36-hour limit.

The superintendent must be satisfied that an offence being investigated is an 'indictable offence' and that there is not sufficient evidence to charge, *and* the investigation is being conducted diligently and expeditiously, *and* that the person's detention is necessary to secure and preserve evidence or obtain evidence by questioning (s. 42 of the Police and Criminal Evidence Act 1984).

The extension of a person's detention must be made *within 24 hours* of the relevant time. Also, the extension cannot be granted before *at least two reviews* have been carried out by the reviewing inspector.

Although reviews are normally carried out after six and nine hours, they can be conducted earlier. Section 42(4) is deliberately worded so that the focus is not on the length of time a person has been in custody, but on how many reviews have been conducted.

A superintendent could authorise an extension in these circumstances but would have to wait until a second review had been conducted.

As STIRLING was arrested for a summary offence, no extension beyond the 24-hour period of initial detention can be made; answers A, B and C are therefore incorrect.

Evidence and Procedure, para. 2.6.18

Answer 6.15

Answer **D** — A superintendent may authorise a person's detention without charge for a maximum of 36 hours (s. 42 of the Police and Criminal Evidence Act 1984). Any further periods of detention must be authorised by a magistrate.

A magistrate may initially authorise detention for 36 hours (s. 43). However, this period may be extended by 24 hours upon further application (s. 44), which means that a magistrate may authorise a maximum detention period of 60 hours. A person may not be detained for longer than 96 hours in total without being charged or released. Answers A, B and C are therefore incorrect.

Evidence and Procedure, para. 2.6.18

Answer 6.16

Answer **A** — If an officer of at least inspector rank considers that a particular solicitor or firm of solicitors is persistently sending probationary representatives who are unsuited to provide legal advice, he/she should inform an officer of at least superintendent rank, who may wish to take the matter up with the Solicitors Regulation Authority. Therefore answer A is the correct answer—answers B, C and D are incorrect as the rank required is superintendent and the wording is may not must.

Evidence and Procedure, para. 2.6.11

Answer 6.17

Answer **B** — When a person is arrested under the provisions of the Criminal Justice Act 2003, which allow a person to be re-tried after being acquitted of a serious offence provided a further prosecution has not been precluded by the Court of Appeal, an officer of the rank of superintendent or above who has not been directly involved in the investigation is responsible for determining whether the evidence is sufficient to charge; answers A, C and D are therefore incorrect.

Evidence and Procedure, para. 2.6.19

Answer 6.18

Answer **D** — Under s. 42(1) of the Police and Criminal Evidence Act 1984, detention can only be authorised beyond 24 hours and up to a maximum of 36 hours from the relevant time if:

- an offence being investigated is an 'indictable offence'; *and*
- an officer of the rank of superintendent or above is responsible for the station at which the person is detained (referred to here as the authorising officer); *and*
- that senior officer is satisfied that:
  - there is not sufficient evidence to charge; *and*
  - the investigation is being conducted diligently and expeditiously; *and*
  - the person's detention is necessary to secure or preserve evidence relating to the offence or to obtain such evidence by questioning that person.

The grounds for this continuing detention are the same as those when the custody officer made the initial decision to detain, with the additional requirements that the case has been conducted diligently and expeditiously. It is suggested that Art. 5 of the European Convention requires this to be a consideration at all times of detention as a person's right to freedom is one of his/her human rights and any unnecessary periods of detention might be considered actionable. To be able to satisfy the senior officer of this, it will be necessary for the custody record to be available for inspection and details of what inquiries have been made, and evidence that the investigation has been moving at a pace that will satisfy the senior officer that the inquiries should not already have been completed. Code C, para. 15.2A outlines issues to be considered before extending the period of juveniles and mentally vulnerable persons.

The authorising officer (which here must be an officer of the rank of superintendent or above who is responsible for the station at which the person is detained) can authorise detention up to a maximum of 36 hours from the 'relevant time' of detention. The period can be shorter than this and can then be further authorised by that officer or any other officer of the rank of superintendent or above who is responsible for the station at which the person is detained to allow the period to be further extended up to the maximum 36-hour period (s. 42(2)). This section outlines that the officer responsible for the station holding the detainee includes a superintendent or above who, in accordance with his/her force operational policy or police regulations, is given that responsibility on a temporary basis whilst the appointed long-term holder is off duty or otherwise unavailable. So, although the superintendent in charge of the city centre police station is clearly the person defined by this section, the Code allows for eventualities where he/she is absent. It would be wrong to bring forward reviews and authorise extensions some time before the clock runs out to accommodate someone going on leave; answers A and B are therefore incorrect.

The extension of a person's detention by a superintendent or above must be made within 24 hours of the relevant time and cannot be made before at least two reviews have been carried out by a review officer under s. 40 of the 1984 Act (i.e. those normally carried out by an inspector) (s. 42(4)) (Code C, para. 15.2); answer C is therefore incorrect.

Evidence and Procedure, para. 2.6.18

Answer 6.19

Answer **D** — While a person is in police detention before charge, his/her detention must be reviewed by an officer of the rank of inspector or above (inspector reviews).

This review acts as another safeguard to protect the detained person's right to be detained for only such periods as are necessary to allow for the investigation of an offence. Review officer for the purposes of ss. 40 and 40A of the 1984 Act means, in the case of a person arrested but not charged, an officer of at least inspector rank not directly involved in the investigation and, if a person has been arrested and charged, the custody officer.

The detention of persons in police custody not subject to the statutory review should still be reviewed periodically as a matter of good practice. The purpose of such reviews is to check that the particular power under which a detainee is held continues to apply, that any associated conditions are complied with and to make sure that appropriate action is taken to deal with any changes. This includes the detainee's prompt release when the power no longer applies, or his/her transfer if the power requires the detainee to be taken elsewhere as soon as the necessary arrangements are made. Examples include persons arrested on warrant because they failed to answer bail to appear at court. This review would be carried out by the custody officer not an inspector; answers A and C are therefore incorrect. The review would be carried out periodically not at set times therefore answer B is incorrect.

Evidence and Procedure, para. 2.6.18

Answer 6.20

Answer **B** — Under s. 54(9) of the Police and Criminal Evidence Act 1984, the constable carrying out a search must be of the same sex as the person searched. Section 54 does not prohibit a constable of the opposite sex from being present at a search, provided it is not a strip search or an intimate search. Answer C is therefore incorrect.

Because of the prohibition referred to previously, under s. 54(9), a constable may *not* search a person of the opposite sex, whether during an ordinary search, a strip search or an intimate search. Answers A and D are therefore incorrect.

Evidence and Procedure, para. 2.6.9

Answer 6.21

Answer **C** — If a decision is taken to charge the detained person, Code C, para. 16 sets out the procedures to be followed by the custody officer. When a detained person is charged with or informed that he/she may be prosecuted for an offence, para. 16.2 requires him/her to be cautioned. The caution varies slightly from that when arrested or interviewed and is as follows:

You do not have to say anything. But it may harm your defence if you do not mention now something which you later rely on in court. Anything you do say may be given in evidence.

This caution should not be used in circumstances where the detained person has been denied access to a solicitor, in which case the following caution should be used:

You do not have to say anything, but anything you do say may be given in evidence.

This is answer C; answers A, B and D are therefore incorrect.

Evidence and Procedure, paras 2.6.19, 2.8.5

Answer 6.22

Answer **A** — An intimate search may be authorised by an inspector and consists of the physical examination of a person's bodily orifices *other than the mouth*. The physical examination of a person's mouth is *not* classed as an intimate search, and may be authorised by a custody officer for the same reasons as a strip search. Answers B and C are incorrect as the search in the scenario does not amount to an intimate search.

An *intimate search* may be conducted only by a medical practitioner (or registered nurse) at medical premises, where the purpose of the search is to discover a Class A drug. Other *intimate searches* may be conducted at the custody office by police officers (provided all the criteria are met). Answer D is therefore incorrect for this reason.

Evidence and Procedure, para. 2.6.20

Answer 6.23

Answer **C** — At least *two light meals* and *one main meal* shall be offered in any period of 24 hours. Answers A, B and D are therefore incorrect. Drinks should be provided at meal times and upon reasonable request between meal times (PACE Code C, para. 8.6). Meals should so far as practicable be offered at recognised meal times.

Evidence and Procedure, para. 2.6.13

Answer 6.24

Answer **B** — Sections 38 and 39 of the Police Reform Act 2002 provide certain police powers for police authority employees. This recognises that many of the functions that were traditionally carried out by police officers are now performed by accredited (and trained) staff, and gives statutory footing to their actions. Part of this group are detention officers, and they are given power to carry out most of the functions that were previously given only to police officers. It includes taking non-intimate samples; answers C and D are therefore incorrect. By virtue of s. 38(8) of the Police Reform Act 2002, detention officers have the same power to use *reasonable* force that is given to police officers in the execution of the same duties; answer A is therefore incorrect.

Evidence and Procedure, para. 2.6.3

Answer 6.25

Answer **B** — In the scenario, HURTY has not been arrested for a 'local offence' therefore the relevant time is the time he arrived at a police station in the police area where he was wanted (not just the time he arrived in that force's area; therefore, answer C is incorrect) *or* 24 hours after arrest, whichever is the earliest. He was arrested at 10 am on Saturday and arrived at the station at 11.30 am on the Sunday, therefore the relevant time is 10 am on the Sunday (by applying the formula, and noting that 10 am is in fact earlier than 11.30 am!). Answer D is therefore incorrect. Had HURTY been questioned by Margate police about the burglary, the relevant time would have been 10.30 am on the Saturday (time of arrival at local station); but as he was not questioned, answer A is incorrect.

Evidence and Procedure, para. 2.6.17.1

Answer 6.26

Answer **C** — Section 41(2)(ca) of the Police and Criminal Evidence Act 1984 states that when a person has been bailed under s. 30A of the Act, his/her relevant time will be the time that he/she arrives at the station (2.30 pm in the scenario). Answers A, B and D are incorrect for this reason.

Evidence and Procedure, para. 2.6.17.1

Answer 6.27

Answer **B** — Any information that is available about the detained person should be considered in deciding whether to request a medical examination. This does not apply to minor ailments or injuries which do not need attention. However, all such ailments or injuries must be recorded in the custody record and any doubt must be resolved in favour of calling the appropriate health care professional. The custody officer must also consider the need for clinical attention in relation to those suffering the effects of alcohol or drugs. Therefore, the custody officer must take into account *any* information about a person's health, whether it comes from the detainee, the arresting officer or any other source. Answer A is therefore incorrect. Whether or not the detainee displayed symptoms of illness is immaterial and therefore answer C is incorrect. Also, the fact that the detainee's sister failed to mention whether or not the person was taking medication or seeking medical help is also immaterial and answer D is therefore incorrect.

Evidence and Procedure, para. 2.6.14

Answer 6.28

Answer **D** — According to the PACE Codes of Practice, Code C, para. 2.1A:

> A person is deemed to be 'at a police station' for these purposes if they are within the boundary of any building or enclosed yard which forms part of that police station.

This definition is far wider than merely inside a police station (and answer C is therefore incorrect) or within the confines of a custody office (and answer B is incorrect). It is important to note this addition to the Codes of Practice, because the time the person arrives at the police station forms the basis of a detainee's relevant time and could have an effect later in the person's detention when investigating officers are seeking extensions. It should also be noted that since many custody offices have CCTV cameras fitted, the accuracy of such information is crucial in case of challenges. Answer A is completely wrong, as a person may be waiting in a police vehicle in a yard outside a busy custody office for some time and this will count towards their overall detention time.

Evidence and Procedure, para. 2.6.7

Answer 6.29

Answer **D** — The situation in this question is covered by PACE Code C, para. 6.5A which states:

> In the case of a juvenile, an appropriate adult should consider whether legal advice from a solicitor is required. If the juvenile indicates that they do not want legal advice, the appropriate adult has the right to ask for a solicitor to attend if this would be in the best interests of the person. However, the detained person cannot be forced to see the solicitor if he is adamant that he does not wish to do so.

As can be seen from this paragraph, a juvenile cannot be made to speak with a legal representative even if this is in his/her best interests, regardless of his/her age or the local Youth Offending Team policy. Answers A and C are therefore incorrect. The appropriate adult *does* have the right to ask for a solicitor to attend if it is in the best interests of the detainee (and answer B is therefore incorrect); however, this right does not extend to forcing the juvenile to speak to the solicitor once he/she has arrived at the custody office.

Evidence and Procedure, para. 2.6.11

Answer 6.30

Answer **B** — PACE Code C, para. 3.4 states that the custody officer shall note on the custody record any comment the detainee makes in relation to the arresting officer's account but shall not invite comment. Therefore answer A is incorrect as is answer D. Discretion does not factor, making answer C incorrect.

Evidence and Procedure, para. 2.6.8

Answer 6.31

Answer **C** — The maximum period a person may be detained without charge under PACE is 96 hours, following the granting of an extension by the magistrates' court. Answers A, B and D are therefore incorrect.

Evidence and Procedure, para. 2.6.17

Answer 6.32

Answer **D** — The standard detention time is 24 hours from the relevant time so, all things being equal, the detention time will end at 10 am on Wednesday.

If a detained person is taken to hospital for medical treatment, the time at hospital and the period spent travelling to and from the hospital does not count towards the relevant time unless the person is asked questions for the purpose of obtaining evidence about an offence. This applies only where questions are actually asked not intended; answer A is therefore incorrect. Also note that the clock would effectively be 'off' from the moment travelling to the hospital begins until it ends. In this scenario, that is from 4 pm to 10 pm. This is six hours off the clock, effectively six hours added to 10 am, making it 4 pm on Wednesday; answers A, B and C are therefore incorrect.

Where questioning takes place, this period would count towards the relevant time and therefore the custody officer must be informed of it (s. 41(6) of PACE).

Evidence and Procedure, para. 2.6.17.1

Answer 6.33

Answer **C** — If a solicitor arrives at the station to see a suspect, the suspect must be asked whether he/she would like to see the solicitor *regardless of what legal advice has already been received* and regardless of whether or not the advice was requested by the suspect; answers B and D are therefore incorrect (PACE Code C, para. 6.15). Note that it is the suspect's choice whether to speak to the solicitor, who has no automatic right of consultation even if summoned by a relative, and answer A is therefore incorrect. However, where a solicitor does arrive at the police station to see a suspect, that suspect has to be told of the solicitor's presence and must be allowed to consult with the solicitor should he/she wish to do so.

Evidence and Procedure, para. 2.6.11

Answer 6.34

Answer **B** — Note that a person in police detention at a hospital must not be questioned without the agreement of a responsible doctor (Code C, para. 14.2) so answers A, C and D are incorrect.

Evidence and Procedure, para. 2.6.16

Answer 6.35

Answer **C** — Code C, para. 13.4 states that where a person makes a statement under caution in a language other than English, the interpreter should record the statement in the language in which it is made, the person must be invited to sign it and an official English translation must be made in due course. There is no provision in the Codes of Practice for the interviewee to write the statement, therefore answers B and D are incorrect. Also, there is no requirement for the statement to be translated immediately, and answer A is therefore incorrect.

Evidence and Procedure, para. 2.6.15

Answer 6.36

Answer **D** — While the situation in the question is unusual, the actions of the police were perfectly legal. Under PACE Code C, para. 14.2, if a person is in police detention at a hospital he/she may not be questioned without the agreement of a responsible doctor. Note 14A continues: 'if questioning takes place at a hospital under paragraph 14.2, or on the way to or from a hospital, *the period of questioning concerned* counts towards the total period of detention permitted'. Answers A and B are therefore incorrect. Answer C is incorrect because both the interview on the way to the hospital and the interview at the hospital will count towards the overall detention time.

Evidence and Procedure, para. 2.6.16

Answer 6.37

Answer **A** — Provision is made under PACE Code C, para. 6.9 to remove a solicitor from an interview if the interviewer considers a solicitor is acting in such a way that his/her conduct means that the interviewer is unable to put questions to the suspect properly. Further guidance is contained in para. 6.10, which states that the interviewing officer must stop the interview and consult an officer not below superintendent rank, if one is readily available, and otherwise an officer not below inspector rank not connected with the investigation. Since either of these officers may take the decision, answers B and D are incorrect. An officer who takes the decision to exclude a solicitor must be in a position to satisfy the court that the decision was properly made. In order to do this, they may need to witness what is happening. It is not mandatory that the authorising officer witnesses the behaviour (therefore answer C is incorrect); however, it would be advisable to do so in order that an informed decision is reached.

Evidence and Procedure, para. 2.6.11

Answer 6.38

Answer **B** — The right to legal advice is an absolute right, however, once the initial decision is made by the suspect he/she may change his/her mind; if they do so, Code C, para. 6.6(d) applies. If a suspect changes his/her mind, or re-changes it, then the auspices of Code C apply again. An interview can go ahead without a solicitor if an inspector speaks to the suspect about his/her decision and agrees that the reasons outlined are appropriate for the interview to continue but the suspect must agree in writing; answer A is therefore incorrect.

It is immaterial when or how the suspect changes his/her mind. That is why the inspector will speak to the suspect to ensure the suspect understands his/her decision; answers C and D are therefore incorrect.

Evidence and Procedure, para. 2.6.11

Answer 6.39

Answer **D** — A solicitor or appropriate adult must be allowed to consult a detainee's custody record as soon as practicable after their arrival at the station and at any other time whilst the person is detained (Code C, para. 2.4). Arrangements for this access must be agreed with the custody officer and may not unreasonably interfere with the custody officer's duties.

Evidence and Procedure, para. 2.6.14

Answer 6.40

Answer **D** — An intimate search can only be authorised in relation to a person who has been arrested and is in police detention (s. 55(1) of PACE) (see para. 2.6.19.1). An officer may give an authorisation under subs. (1) orally or in writing but, if given orally, it shall be confirmed in writing as soon as practicable (s. 55(3)).

Body orifices other than the mouth may be searched only:

(a) if authorised by an officer of inspector rank or above who has reasonable grounds for believing that the person may have concealed on themselves:
   (i) anything which they could and might use to cause physical injury to themselves or others at the station; or
   (ii) a Class A drug which they intended to supply to another or to export;
   (iii) and the officer has reasonable grounds for believing that an intimate search is the only means of removing those items.

In *Owens* v *Chief Constable of Merseyside* [2021] EWHC 3119 (QB), whilst in custody the detainee having been 'asked' to remove his trousers and underwear was then 'asked to separate his penis and testicles, to pull his foreskin back and then to turn around and lean over, separating his bottom cheeks'. This was to check whether Class A drugs had been secreted in these areas. The question for the court was whether this was a strip search or intimate search. The court found that the definition of 'intimate search' ('the physical examination of a person's body orifices other than the mouth') requires an act of physical intrusion into a body orifice. In this case, the only 'examination' taking place inside the body orifice was 'visual' and therefore was not an intimate search. What matters is the exploration inside the body orifice: where that exploration is physically penetrative, it is 'physical intrusion into the body orifice' and therefore 'some physical examination'. Therefore answers A, B and C are incorrect.

Evidence and Procedure, para. 2.6.22

7 | Identification

QUESTIONS

Question 7.1

Officers are investigating a robbery where a suspect was captured on dashcam fleeing the scene. The suspect claims it could not have been him as he was home alone at the time of the robbery. There are no further eye-witnesses and no forensic evidence linking the suspect to the robbery. A facial mapping expert has been brought in; the suspect has grown a beard since the offence.

In relation to the face mapping expert, which of the following is correct?

A The evidence of the expert will not, in itself, be enough to identify the suspect as being at the scene.

B The face mapping expert can use a reasonably contemporary photograph of the suspect to compare to the image on the dashcam.

C The face mapping expert can use a photograph of the suspect taken at or about the time of the offence only to compare to the image on the dashcam.

D The face mapping expert can use a photograph of the suspect taken now to compare to the image on the dashcam.

Question 7.2

CAPLE is a witness to an armed robbery and is being interviewed by a police officer. CAPLE provides a handwritten note that she wrote down of the description of the suspect she had seen commit the robbery. The writing on the note is very clear and outlines in detail the description of the suspect.

In relation to this, which of the following is correct?

A The officer should now record that description in her pocket notebook, this will then be a record of that first description.

B The officer should now record that description in the witness's statement, this will then be a record of that first description.
C The officer must ask the witness to time and date and then sign the handwritten note as the first description.
D The officer should retain the handwritten note as this is the first description.

Question 7.3

Inspector HALES is carrying out an identification procedure and has a copy of the first description of the suspect as obtained from an eye-witness. The suspect is represented by a solicitor.

What should the inspector do with this record?
A The inspector must give it to the solicitor prior to the identification procedure taking place.
B The inspector must give it to the suspect or his/her solicitor prior to the identification procedure taking place.
C The inspector must, where practicable, give it only to the solicitor prior to the identification procedure taking place.
D The inspector must, where practicable, give it to the suspect or his/her solicitor prior to the identification procedure taking place.

Question 7.4

Constable DUFFY was on mobile patrol and was accompanied by a colleague from the Dutch police. While stationary at traffic lights, a car pulled alongside them. Constable DUFFY recognised the driver as NANCARROW whom she knew was a disqualified driver. In the vehicle was NANCARROW's wife, whom the officer also recognised. The vehicles were next to each other for no more than 30 seconds, and NANCARROW's vehicle made off and was not traced. NANCARROW was arrested some time later and denied being the driver and demanded an identification parade. The Dutch officer is now with another force several hundred miles away.

In relation to identification procedures, which of the following is correct?
A An identification must be held with Constable DUFFY as an eye-witness, it is not practical to hold one for the Dutch officer.
B An identification procedure should be held with the Dutch officer as an eyewitness, there would be no useful purpose in having Constable DUFFY as a witness.

C An identification procedure should be held with both Constable DUFFY and the Dutch officer as eye-witnesses.

D An identification procedure need not be held as it is not practical to hold one for the Dutch officer and there would be no useful purpose in having Constable DUFFY as an eye-witness.

Question 7.5

PRYCE was approached by three men and robbed of his wallet. This was witnessed by someone who observed the suspects at length; the eye-witness could describe the age of the men and the clothes that they were wearing but does not give any further descriptions of them. Three men are arrested later and the police are considering whether an identification parade should be held with the witness as the men deny being the robbers although they accept that they were at the scene when it took place.

In these circumstances, should an identification procedure be held?

A Yes, this is an issue of identification and it is disputed; a procedure should be held.

B Yes, even though this is only an issue of participation, a procedure should be held.

C No, the men accept they were at the scene so an identification procedure would not be of any assistance.

D No, as this is identification of clothing and not the suspects, an identification procedure would not be of any assistance.

Question 7.6

Police officers are dealing with a murder inquiry during which there was significant publicity to identify a suspect. The suspect has been identified and an identification procedure is being considered by the police.

What is the requirement on the police in relation to material released by them to the press for publicity purposes?

A The material need only be retained and disclosed in accordance with the relevant codes of the Criminal Procedure and Investigations Act 1996.

B The material must be shown to either the suspect or his/her solicitor prior to any identification procedure taking place.

C The material must be shown, where practicable, to either the suspect or his/her solicitor prior to any identification procedure taking place.

D The material need not be retained by the police or shown to either the suspect or his/her solicitor as it has already been in the public domain.

Question 7.7

CURBISHLEY was arrested on suspicion of burglary as fingerprint identification from the scene of the crime was available. CURBISHLEY initially denied the offence, and the taking of his fingerprints was authorised to prove or disprove his involvement in the offence and taken for that purpose. Following further comparison and further interviews, CURBISHLEY admitted the offence. CURBISHLEY has been charged and the officer in charge of the case wishes to take his fingerprints. CURBISHLEY refuses this request.

Which of the following statements is true?

A As CURBISHLEY has been charged, his fingerprints can be taken without his consent.

B As CURBISHLEY has been charged, his fingerprints can be taken only with his consent.

C As CURBISHLEY has refused, an inspector's authority, in writing, is required.

D As CURBISHLEY has refused, an inspector's authority, which can be oral or written, is required.

Question 7.8

GRAVES does not have a criminal record and has been arrested and charged with a recordable qualifying offence; he appears at court and is found not guilty. When he was in custody, his fingerprints were taken and he is wondering now whether these fingerprints will be destroyed.

In relation to this, which of the following is correct?

A As he has been arrested and charged with a recordable qualifying offence, his fingerprints can be retained for five years for the prevention and detection of crime.

B As he has been found not guilty of the recordable qualifying offence he was charged with, the fingerprints must be destroyed.

C His fingerprints will be retained for three years plus an extra two years if an extension is granted by a district judge.

D If he was charged with a minor offence, then his fingerprints will be retained for ten years.

Question 7.9

DC CHARLSON is the officer in the case for an offence of rape alleged against MARLEY. DC CHARLSON wishes to obtain a penile swab sample from MARLEY who is now in custody for that rape offence. Section 62 of the Police and Criminal Evidence Act 1984 allows for the taking from a suspect of intimate and non-intimate samples.

Would the taking of this penile swab from MARLEY be classified as an intimate sample?

A Yes, this is an intimate sample even though it is not a body orifice.

B Yes, as the legislation states that the penis is in effect a body orifice.

C No, as intimate samples are samples of blood, semen or any other tissue fluid, urine or pubic hair.

D No, as a non-intimate sample is described as a swab taken from any part of a person's body including the mouth but not any other body orifice.

Question 7.10

McGREGOR is a 16-year-old boy who has been arrested following an allegation of rape against him. When he was brought into custody, a member of social services was called to act as appropriate adult, however, they left when the police said the interviews would be held in several hours' time. The officer in charge of the investigation now wants to take an intimate sample which would require the removal of the suspect's clothing. McGREGOR agrees to give the sample and states that he does not want the social worker to be present. The social worker is phoned and agrees that she does not need to be present when the juvenile's clothes are removed.

Can the police now lawfully remove the juvenile's clothes to obtain an intimate sample?

A Yes, the suspect has agreed and indicated he does not wish to have an appropriate adult present.

B Yes, the suspect has agreed and indicated he does not wish to have an appropriate adult present, and the appropriate adult agrees.

C No, as the appropriate adult was not present with the juvenile when he elected not to have an appropriate adult present.

D No, as an appropriate adult would have to be present at all times when an intimate sample is taken, provided they are of the same sex.

Question 7.11

HIGGINS was arrested for an offence of theft and a mouth swab was taken lawfully from him. He was released from custody and later the sample taken proved to be unsuitable or insufficient.

In relation to obtaining another sample, which of the following is true?

A It must be retaken within six months of the date of release.

B It must be retaken within six months of the officer being told it was unsuitable or insufficient.

C It must be retaken within one year of the date of release.

D It must be retaken within one year of the officer being told it was unsuitable or insufficient.

Question 7.12

DC YALE and DC ROW are dealing with HICKS for an offence of sexual assault by penetration. HICKS has been released under investigation but DC YALE wishes to seek to obtain further intimate samples and states, incorrectly, that these can be obtained with the consent of HICKS alone. DC ROW informs DC YALE that intimate samples may be taken from persons in police detention or, in certain circumstances, from persons who are not in police detention but only with the relevant authority.

In relation to the authority needed for the taking of such samples, which of the following is true?

A Inspector's authority in detention; superintendent's authority not in detention.

B Inspector's authority irrespective of whether the person is in detention or not.

C Superintendent's authority irrespective of whether the person is in detention or not.

D Superintendent's authority in detention; inspector's authority not in detention.

Question 7.13

WILTORD was arrested by DC COLE for an assault. He was released on bail for an identification procedure and his fingerprints were taken prior to his release. On the day that he was due to answer bail, WILTORD's brother, who was similar in appearance, attended the station instead of WILTORD, in an attempt to confuse witnesses. However, after the brother had been booked in by the custody officer, DC COLE suspected that he was not the person who had been released on bail.

DC COLE contacted the duty inspector by telephone and asked for permission to obtain fingerprints from WILTORD's brother because of his suspicions.

Would the duty inspector be able to authorise such a request in these circumstances?

A No, this power is only given to a court when a person has been charged with an offence.

B No, this power is only given to an inspector where a person has been charged with an offence.

C Yes, but the fingerprints may be taken only when the inspector has provided written authority.

D Yes, and the fingerprints may be taken immediately.

Question 7.14

HOPE was stationary in his car when he was approached by two men who threatened him with knives and stole his wallet. The men did not disguise their appearance and had local accents. Shaken by the experience, HOPE visited his sister who suggested he searched Facebook to see if he recognised anyone. After several days, he saw one of the men had an account and had posted on the day of the robbery that he had come into some money.

In relation to this identification, which of the following is correct?

A The suspect would now be a known suspect and no further identification procedure should be used.

B This is now a recognition case and no further identification procedure should be used.

C The police should obtain as much evidence as possible to establish how the identification was made using Facebook.

D The only option open to the police would be to show photographs to HOPE in controlled conditions following the procedure laid down in Annex E of Code D of PACE.

Question 7.15

Constable GILES is being tutored by Constable HADLOW. Constable HADLOW wishes to check Constable GILES's knowledge of 'intimate' and 'non-intimate samples' in line with PACE Code D, para. 6.1.

Which of the following should Constable GILES identify as a 'non-intimate' sample?

A A skin impression other than a fingerprint.

B A sample of urine.

C A blood sample.

D A dental impression.

Question 7.16

Police officers have arrested TIMSON, who is 12 years of age, for a burglary (a recordable offence). The officers wish to take a footwear impression as part of their investigation of this offence.

In relation to this, which of the following is correct?

A This could only be done with written consent from TIMSON and his parents.

B This could only be done with the written consent of TIMSON's parents.

C This can be done without consent as he has been arrested for a recordable offence.

D This cannot be done as he is under the age of 14 years.

Question 7.17

FELICE was arrested for an offence of theft but will not be charged as there was insufficient evidence. Police wish to take FELICE's photograph for future use while she is still in police detention.

In relation to taking the photograph, which of the following is correct?

A The photograph can be taken without FELICE's consent and used for identification procedures.

B The photograph can be taken but only if FELICE gives her permission.

C The photograph can be taken without FELICE's consent but cannot be used for identification procedures.

D The photograph cannot be taken as FELICE has not been charged or reported for a recordable offence.

Question 7.18

POTTER has been arrested on suspicion of criminal damage and is in a very bad mood. On arrival at custody, he refuses to answer any questions, engage with any requests or instructions and stares at the wall in silence. The custody officer has authorised POTTER's detention and seeks to have POTTER searched in order to ascertain his identity which can be done without the consent of the detainee, under s. 54A of the Police and Criminal Evidence Act 1984.

Who, out of the following, can correctly give such authorisation?

A An officer of at least the rank of superintendent only, either orally or in writing, provided it is confirmed in writing as soon as practicable.

B An officer of at least the rank of inspector before charge, or a custody officer after charge, either orally or in writing, provided it is confirmed in writing as soon as practicable.

C An officer of at least the rank of inspector, either orally or in writing, provided it is confirmed in writing as soon as practicable.

D An officer of at least the rank of inspector, and permission may only be given in writing.

Question 7.19

DING was arrested for being found drunk in a public place. He was so intoxicated that when he arrived at the station he was placed in a cell after being searched and fell asleep immediately. DING had nothing in his property which would have assisted in identifying him, therefore the arresting officer asked the custody officer whether DING could be examined without his consent, while he was asleep, to establish if he had any tattoos that might assist in identifying him.

Could an examination be authorised without DING's consent, under s. 54A(1)(b) of the Police and Criminal Evidence Act 1984, in these circumstances?

A Yes, because it was not practicable to obtain his consent.

B No, as the purpose of the examination must be to photograph any tattoos.

C Yes, if an officer of the rank of inspector or above gave his/her authority.

D No, as DING has not been given an opportunity to identify himself.

Question 7.20

OGINSKY (aged 16 years) has been arrested for an offence of robbery (a recordable offence) and has been transported to the custody block of a designated police station. DC PIGDEN (the officer in the case) interviews OGINSKY in the presence of FARROW (who is OGINSKY's uncle and acting as an appropriate adult). During the interview, DC PIGDEN tells OGINSKY that he wishes to obtain footwear impressions from him (under s. 61A of the Police and Criminal Evidence Act 1984) and asks for his consent—OGINSKY refuses.

Can DC PIGDEN obtain footwear samples from OGINSKY in these circumstances?

A No, as footwear samples can only be obtained from a person in police detention with their written consent.

B Yes, and DC PIGDEN can use force to obtain them if necessary.

C No, unless FARROW provides written consent for DC PIGDEN to obtain footwear impressions from OGINSKY.

D Yes, if the impressions are necessary to prove or disprove OGINSKY's involvement in the robbery offence.

ANSWERS

Answer 7.1

Answer **B** — A suitably qualified expert with facial mapping skills giving opinion evidence of identification based on a comparison between images from the scene and a reasonably contemporary photograph (answers C and D are therefore incorrect) of the defendant could be given so long as the image and photograph were available to the jury.

In *R v Purlis* [2017] EWCA Crim 1134, a dashboard camera captured a robber departing the scene in the car. The court allowed a facial mapping expert to give evidence that by comparing images from the dashcam with photographs of the suspect he could identify features which, taken together, lent powerful support to the contention that the images were of the same man. This followed the case of *R v Atkins* [2010] 1 Cr App R 8, where the court held that it is important to approach the evidence of facial mapping with caution. That does not mean that you cannot rely on the expert evidence; simply, that it needs to be considered with care. The court went on to say that an expert who spends many years studying this kind of evidence can properly form an opinion as to the significance of what he/she has found; answer A is therefore incorrect.

Evidence and Procedure, para. 2.7.4.13

Answer 7.2

Answer **D** — PACE Code D, para. 3.1 states:

A record shall be made of the suspect's description as first given by the eye-witness. This record must:

(a) be made and kept in a form which enables details of that description to be accurately produced from it, in a visible and legible form, which can be given to the suspect or the suspect's solicitor in accordance with this Code...

So as it is legible then the handwritten note is the first description of the suspect and should be retained by the officer; there is nothing in the Code that states it needs to be signed and timed; answer C is therefore incorrect.

Although this description may be in the officer's PNB and the witness's statement, neither of these will be the record of first description; answers A and B are therefore incorrect.

Evidence and Procedure, para. 2.7.4.2

Answer 7.3

Answer **D** — Code D requires that a first description provided of a person suspected of a crime (regardless of the time it was given) must be recorded (para. 3.1) and that a copy of the record should, where practicable (answers A and B are therefore incorrect), be given to the defence before certain procedures such as identification parades are carried out.

This record must be made and kept in a form which enables details of that description to be accurately produced from it, in a visible and legible form (Code D, para. 3.1), which can be given to the suspect or the suspect's solicitor; answer C is therefore incorrect.

Evidence and Procedure, para. 2.7.4.2

Answer 7.4

Answer **B** — PACE Code D, paras 3.12 and 3.13 outline circumstances in which an eye-witness identification procedure must be held:

Whenever:

(a) an eye-witness has identified a suspect or purported to have identified them; or
(b) there is an eye-witness available who expresses an ability to identify the suspect; or
(c) there is a reasonable chance of an eye-witness being able to identify the suspect, and the eye-witness in (a) to (c) has not been given an opportunity to identify the suspect in any of the procedures set out in *paragraphs 3.5* to *3.10*, then an identification procedure shall be held if the suspect disputes being the person the eye-witness claims to have seen on a previous occasion.

Code D, para. 3.12(b) provides that there is no need to go through any of the identification procedures where it is not practicable or it would serve no useful purpose in proving or disproving whether the suspect was involved in committing the offence. Examples would be where it is not in dispute that the suspect is already well known to the witness who claims to have seen the suspect commit the crime or where there is no reasonable possibility that a witness would be able to make an identification.

In this scenario, if an identification procedure had been held, the officer would have picked NANCARROW out as the driver (as she knew not only him but also another occupant of the car), making an identification procedure somewhat pointless, with no useful purpose; answers A and C are therefore incorrect.

However, attempts should be made to have the Dutch officer as a witness. Although several hundred miles away, it is still practical; answers A, C and D are therefore incorrect.

Evidence and Procedure, para. 2.7.4.4

Answer 7.5

Answer **D** — Code D, para. 3.12(ii) provides that there is no need to go through any of the identification procedures where it is not practicable or it would serve no useful purpose in proving or disproving whether the suspect was involved in committing the offence.

It is important to consider the distinction between identification of a suspect and the suspect's clothing or other features. In *D* v *DPP* (1998), The Times, 7 August, a witness had observed two youths for a continuous period of five to six minutes and then informed the police of what he had seen, describing the age of the youths and the clothes that they were wearing. The court held that there had not been an identification within the terms of the Codes of Practice because the witness had at no stage identified the defendant or the co-accused. He had described only their clothing and their approximate ages, and the police, acting on that information, had made the arrests. An identification parade could have served no useful purpose since the clothing would have been changed and those persons used for the parade would have been the same approximate age; answers A and B are therefore incorrect.

This point was further supported in *R* v *Haynes* [2004] EWCA Crim 390, where the Court of Appeal held that as a practical point the identification parade, whether or not the suspect was regarded as a known or unknown suspect, was of little value where the witness identified the suspect by clothing and not by recognition of the suspect's features. An identification parade would have provided little assistance.

Even accepting that they were at the scene, should a witness actually have described them then an identification parade may have had to have been held as it was their criminal participation that was disputed; answer C is therefore incorrect.

Evidence and Procedure, paras 2.7.4.4 to 2.7.4.5

Answer 7.6

Answer **C** — Nothing in Code D of the PACE Codes of Practice inhibits showing films or photographs to the public through the national or local media, or to police officers for the purposes of recognition and tracing suspects.

When a broadcast or publication is made, a copy of the relevant material released to the media for the purposes of recognising or tracing the suspect, shall be kept.

The suspect or his/her solicitor shall be allowed to view such material before any eye-witness identification procedure is carried out, provided it is practicable; answers A, B and D are therefore incorrect.

Evidence and Procedure, para. 2.7.4.16

Answer 7.7

Answer **B** — Naturally, a person can consent to having his/her fingerprints taken at any time; the law deals with occasions where such consent is missing. Such cases are covered by s. 61 of the Police and Criminal Evidence Act 1984. Under s. 61(4), the fingerprints of a person detained at a police station may be taken without that person's consent in the following two circumstances:

(4) The fingerprints of a person detained at a police station may be taken without the appropriate consent if—
  (a) he has been charged with a recordable offence or informed that he will be reported for such an offence; and
  (b) he has not had his fingerprints taken in the course of the investigation of the offence by the police.

As his fingerprints have already been taken, they cannot be taken again without consent or an inspector's authority; answers A, C and D are therefore incorrect. Although in certain circumstances fingerprints can be taken without consent, this question is clearly aimed at where fingerprints will be taken with consent. Clearly, fingerprints taken without consent will only apply where consent has been sought and not given.

Evidence and Procedure, para. 2.7.5

Answer 7.8

Answer **C** — As GRAVES has been charged but not convicted of a recordable qualifying offence, his fingerprints will be retained for three years plus a two-year extension if granted by a district judge, making answers A, B and D incorrect.

Evidence and Procedure, para. 2.7.13

Answer 7.9

Answer **A** — The definition of an intimate sample is:

- a sample of blood, semen or any other tissue fluid, urine or pubic hair;
- a dental impression;
- a swab taken from any part of a person's genitals or from a person's body orifice other than the mouth.

The definition of a non-intimate sample is:

- a sample of hair, other than pubic hair, which includes hair plucked with the root;
- a sample taken from a nail or from under a nail;
- a swab taken from any part of a person's body including the mouth but not any other body orifice other than a part from which a swab taken would be an intimate sample;
- saliva;
- a skin impression which means any record, other than a fingerprint, which is a record, in any form and produced by any method, of a skin pattern and other physical characteristics or features of the whole, or any part of, a person's foot or of any other part of his/her body.

So a swab from a person's penis would be an intimate sample and the Serious Organised Crime and Police Act 2005 has extended the definition beyond a 'body orifice', although it has not gone as far as declaring the penis to be a body orifice; answer B is therefore incorrect. Answer D is almost correct, apart from the caveat in the definition that states 'a swab taken from any part of a person's body including the mouth but not any other body orifice other than a part from which a swab taken would be an intimate sample'; answers C and D are therefore incorrect as a penile swab is an intimate sample.

Evidence and Procedure, para. 2.7.7

Answer 7.10

Answer **C** — PACE Code D, para. 6.9 states that when clothing needs to be removed in circumstances likely to cause embarrassment to the person, no person of the opposite sex who is not a registered medical practitioner or registered health care professional shall be present (unless in the case of a juvenile, mentally disordered or mentally vulnerable person, that person specifically requests the presence of an appropriate adult of the opposite sex who is readily available) nor shall anyone whose presence is unnecessary. However, in the case of a juvenile this is subject to the over-riding proviso that such a removal of clothing may take place in the absence of the appropriate adult only if the juvenile signifies in their presence that they prefer the adult's absence and the adult agrees.

Clearly, as consent is needed to take a sample, the use of force would be inappropriate.

In the case of a juvenile, the appropriate adult need not be present if the juvenile signifies (in the presence of the appropriate adult) that he/she prefers his/her absence and the appropriate adult agrees; as the agreement of the adult is required, answer A is incorrect.

In this scenario, although the juvenile did not want an appropriate adult present and the adult agreed, this conversation would have had to take place with the adult present, which she was not; answer B is therefore incorrect. An adult does not have to be present when an intimate sample is taken, provided both the juvenile and the adult agree; answer D is therefore incorrect.

Evidence and Procedure, para. 2.7.7.4

Answer 7.11

Answer **B** — By s. 63(3ZA) of the Police and Criminal Evidence Act 1984, a non-intimate sample may be taken without the appropriate consent from a person from whom a non-intimate sample was taken in the course of the investigation but that sample was not suitable or proved insufficient. The requirement *may not be made more than six months from the day the investigating officer was informed that the sample previously taken was not suitable or proved insufficient*, making answers A, C and D therefore incorrect.

Evidence and Procedure, para. 2.7.7.4

Answer 7.12

Answer **B** — Section 62 of the Police and Criminal Evidence Act 1984 sets out police powers in relation to intimate samples, and the circumstances under which they may be obtained. They are subject to the consent of the person, as well as author-isation by the appropriate police officer—that authorisation will be from a police officer of inspector rank or above (as outlined in Code D, para. 6.2); therefore, answers A, C and D are incorrect.

Evidence and Procedure, para. 2.7.7.2

Answer 7.13

Answer **D** — An officer of at least the rank of inspector (or the court) may authorise taking the fingerprints of a person who has answered bail at a court or police station, if the person answering bail has done so on behalf of a person whose fingerprints were taken on a previous occasion and there are reasonable grounds for believing that he/she is not the same person, or the person claims to be a different person from a person whose fingerprints were taken previously (s. 61(4A) of the Police and Criminal Evidence Act 1984).

Since this power relates to a person answering bail at a police station as well as a court, answer A is incorrect. Answers A and B are also incorrect because the power may be utilised before a person has been charged with an offence. The authority to take fingerprints in these circumstances may be given orally or in writing; but if given orally, it must be confirmed in writing as soon as is practicable. Answer C is therefore incorrect.

Evidence and Procedure, para. 2.7.5

Answer 7.14

Answer **C** — If a suspect is 'known' or is 'recognised', there may still be occasions where an identification procedure may need to be followed; answers A and B are therefore incorrect. In *R* v *Alexander and McGill* [2012] EWCA Crim 2768, the victim identified the suspects through their Facebook account pictures. The court observed that identifications done in this way, through the use of Facebook, were likely to arise and it was therefore incumbent upon investigators to take steps to obtain, in as much detail as possible, evidence in relation to the initial identification. In this case, before trial requests were made by the defence for photographs of the other Facebook pages that had been considered by the victim and his sister, so that defendants could consider how their identifications might have been made. This means that showing of photographs in line with Annex E would not be correct and that the police should obtain as much detail as possible as to how the identification was made on social media; answer D is therefore incorrect.

Evidence and Procedure, paras 2.7.4.4, 2.7.4.13

Answer 7.15

Answer **A** — PACE Code D, para. 6.1 provides the following definition of intimate and non-intimate samples:

(a) an 'intimate sample' means:
  - a sample of blood, semen, or any other tissue fluid, urine or pubic hair;
  - a dental impression;
  - a swab taken from any part of a person's genitals or from a person's body orifice other than the mouth.
(b) a 'non-intimate sample' means:
  - a sample of hair, other than pubic hair, which includes hair plucked with the root;
  - a sample taken from a nail or from under a nail;
  - a swab taken from any part of a person's body other than a part from which a swab taken would be an intimate sample;
  - saliva;
  - a skin impression which means any record, other than a fingerprint, which is a record, in any form and produced by any method, of the skin pattern and other physical characteristics or features of the whole, or any part of, a person's foot or of any other part of their body.

Answers B, C and D are all intimate samples. A skin impression which is not a fingerprint is a non-intimate sample.

Evidence and Procedure, para. 2.7.7

Answer 7.16

Answer **C** — Impressions of a person's footwear may be taken in connection with the investigation of an offence only with their consent or if Code D, para. 4.17 applies, which states:

PACE, section 61A, provides power for a police officer to take footwear impressions without consent from any person over the age of ten years who is detained at a police station:

(a) in consequence of being arrested for a recordable offence; or if the detainee has been charged with a recordable offence, or informed they will be reported for such an offence...

No consent is required and the impressions can be taken; answers A, B and D are therefore incorrect.

Evidence and Procedure, para. 2.7.5.3

Answer 7.17

Answer **A** — A person who is detained at a police station or elsewhere than at a police station may be photographed with his/her consent; or if it is withheld or it is not practicable to obtain it, without his/her consent (Code D, para. 5.12(a)). This applies to all persons who are in police detention, and not just those charged or reported for an offence; therefore, answer D is incorrect.

As photographs can be taken without consent, answer B is incorrect. A photograph taken under s. 64A may be used or disclosed only for purposes related to the prevention or detection of crime, the investigation of offences or the conduct of prosecutions by, or on behalf of, police or other law enforcement and prosecuting authorities inside and outside the United Kingdom or the enforcement of any sentence or order made by a court when dealing with an offence. After being so used or disclosed, they may be retained but can only be used or disclosed for the same purposes. This therefore allows the photograph to be used in the preparation of any identification procedure that is being arranged involving the suspect (Code D, para. 3.30); answer C is therefore incorrect.

Evidence and Procedure, para. 2.7.6

Answer 7.18

Answer **C** — The authority to search detainees and examine them to ascertain their identity is contained in s. 54A of the Police and Criminal Evidence Act 1984. An officer of at least the rank of inspector may authorise a person to be searched or examined in order to ascertain if the person has any mark that would tend to identify him/her as a person involved in the commission of an offence, or any mark that would assist in identifying him/her (including showing that he/she is not a particular person). Answers A and B are therefore incorrect. Authority may be given either orally or in writing, provided it is confirmed in writing as soon as practicable (see Code D, para. 5.8). Answer D is therefore incorrect.

Evidence and Procedure, para. 2.7.6

Answer 7.19

Answer **D** — PACE, s. 54A(1), allows a detainee at a police station to be searched or examined or both, to establish:

(a) whether they have any marks, features or injuries that would tend to identify them as a person involved in the commission of an offence and to photograph any identifying marks, see *paragraph 5.5*; or
(b) their identity.

(Code D, para. 5.1)

A search and/or examination to find marks under s. 54A(1)(a) may be carried out without the detainee's consent only if authorised by an officer of at least inspector rank when consent has been withheld or it is not practicable to obtain consent. A search or examination to establish a suspect's identity under s. 54A(1)(b) may be carried out without the detainee's consent, only if authorised by an officer of at least inspector rank *when the detainee has refused to identify themselves or the authorising officer has reasonable grounds for suspecting the person is not who they claim to be.*

The detainee in the scenario would fall within para. 5(1)(b). As DING has not been given the opportunity to identify himself, the use of the power in these circumstances would be inappropriate (correct answer D).

Evidence and Procedure, para. 2.7.6

Answer 7.20

Answer **B** — Code D deals with the process of taking footwear impressions in connection with a criminal investigation. Impressions of a person's footwear may be taken in connection with the investigation of an offence only with their consent or if para. 4.17 applies. If the person is at a police station, consent must be in writing. Paragraph 4.17 states that PACE, s. 61A, provides power for a police officer to take footwear impressions without consent from any person over the age of 10 years who is detained at a police station:

(a) in consequence of being arrested for a recordable offence, or if the detainee has been charged with a recordable offence, or informed they will be reported for such an offence; and

(b) the detainee has not had an impression of their footwear taken in the course of the investigation of the offence unless the previously taken impression is not complete or is not of sufficient quality to allow satisfactory analysis, comparison or matching (whether in the case in question or generally).

This makes answers A and C incorrect (as the consent of DC PIGDEN or FARROW is not required). It is not necessary that the footprints are taken to prove or disprove the detained person's involvement in the offence, making answer D incorrect. Paragraph 4.18 of Code D states that reasonable force may be used, if necessary, to take a footwear impression from a detainee without consent under the power in para. 4.17 (correct answer B). A record must be made as soon as possible of the reason for taking a person's footwear impressions without consent. If force is used, a record shall be made of the circumstances and those present (para. 4.20 of Code D).

Evidence and Procedure, para. 2.7.5.3

8 | Interviews

QUESTIONS

Question 8.1

Constable CAMBLE is on patrol in a vehicle carrying ANPR. A vehicle passes and the ANPR alerts Constable CAMBLE to the fact that the vehicle is reported stolen. The officer stops the vehicle and sees an elderly couple are the only occupants. The officer suspects that the vehicle is not stolen due to the age of the occupants and that some sort of error has occurred in relation to the stolen report about the vehicle. Constable CAMBLE stops the vehicle and says to the driver, 'Who is the vehicle registered to?'

In these circumstances, should the Constable CAMBLE have cautioned the driver as outlined in Code C of the Police and Criminal Evidence Act 1984?

A Yes, as the vehicle is stolen and there are grounds to suspect an offence has been committed.

B Yes, as the vehicle is stolen the officer must caution the driver even if only asking questions about ownership.

C No, as the officer does not suspect the driver of committing an offence, he need not caution him.

D No, questions only to establish ownership of a vehicle never need to be prefaced with a caution.

Question 8.2

Constable HAWKINS is dealing with an offence of theft, where a man is suspected to have been stealing from his mother. The man attends voluntarily at the police station and explains to the police support staff inquiry officer that he is 'there to be interviewed about a theft, but they'll never find where I've hidden the jewellery'.

The man laughed out loud and winked at the inquiry officer. The inquiry officer believed the man to be joking with her.

Was what the man said to the inquiry officer a 'significant statement' as outlined in PACE Code C, para. 11.4A?

A Yes, it appears capable of being used in evidence against him.
B Yes, it was said within the confines of a police station, and to a police officer or police staff.
C No, it was not said to a police officer; police staff are not mentioned in the relevant code.
D No, it is not a confession and does not relate to a direct admission of guilt.

Question 8.3

Police officers have been called by the head teacher of a secondary school to interview a juvenile who has caused damage to school property. The head teacher did not witness the incident but wishes the juvenile to be interviewed on the school premises as the youth is due to sit an extremely important examination in two hours. The parents of the juvenile have been contacted but are unavailable for some time.

Which of the following comments is correct regarding the head teacher acting as an 'appropriate adult'?

A In these circumstances, only the head teacher can be the appropriate adult.
B The head teacher can be the appropriate adult as the parents are not readily available.
C The head teacher can be the appropriate adult provided the parents agree.
D The head teacher will not be able to be the appropriate adult in these circumstances.

Question 8.4

In the early hours of a Sunday morning, intruders were reported in an off-licence and police were called to attend. SYED was found inside the premises and was arrested on suspicion of burglary. Later that day, SYED is being interviewed in relation to burglary and has declined to utilise his right to legal advice. During a break, SYED tells the interviewing officer that he wants to object to the interview being audibly recorded.

What action should the officer now take?

A The officer must allow SYED's objections to be recorded on the audio recording and then switch it off.

B The officer must state on the audio recording that the interview will no longer be recorded and that a written record will now be made and then switch the audio recording off.

C The officer should tell SYED that the objections are required to be recorded and then ask the custody officer to decide whether or not the interview will be audio recorded.

D The officer should state on the audio recording that an objection has been raised; however, it is his/her decision whether to proceed with the audio recording still on.

Question 8.5

Constable HIGGINS has been interviewing BELLFIELD at length about an offence of fraud and is about to start another interview after a break for lunch. BELLFIELD has a legal adviser present during the interview. The officer reminds BELLFIELD that she is under caution but he does not give the caution again.

In relation to this, which of the following is correct in accordance with the Codes of Practice?

A The officer should stop the recording until he has cautioned BELLFIELD again.

B The officer should caution BELLFIELD again as there should be no doubt that she is unaware that she is still under caution.

C The officer has fully complied with the Code in reminding BELLFIELD that she is under caution and there are no other requirements.

D The officer has fully complied with the Code in reminding BELLFIELD that she is under caution as the suspect's solicitor is present at the interview.

Question 8.6

STODDARD has been arrested and is in custody at the police station suspected of a series of rapes; this followed a description obtained from his various victims—a first description was obtained and recorded. The suspect has, in accordance with his rights, asked for his solicitor to be called. Prior to the arrival of his solicitor, STODDARD is examined by the police surgeon and samples obtained. Officers also attend at STODDARD's home address and carry out a search in compliance with s. 18 of the Police and Criminal Evidence Act 1984 and various items are seized as being of evidential value. Prior to the first interview, the interview coordinator is considering what will be disclosed to STODDARD's solicitor.

In relation to the various items obtained, what must be disclosed to the solicitor at this stage of the investigation?

A Only the custody record.

B The custody record and the record of first description.

C The custody record, the record of first description and the details of the items seized.

D At this stage, there is no mandatory disclosure, it is discretionary for the investigating officer.

Question 8.7

Detective Sergeant STROUD is carrying out a visually recorded interview with a suspect for murder. The suspect is a well-known gang member and Detective Sergeant STROUD reasonably believes that disclosing his own name will put him in danger and wishes to hide his identity and sit with his back to the camera. There have been no specific threats made against Detective Sergeant STROUD; however, the gang members have issued a generic warning to any officer concerned in the investigation of the murder.

Would Detective Sergeant STROUD be allowed to use his warrant number and sit with his back to the visual recording device?

A The officer can do this, but must record the reasons for this in the interview.

B The officer can do this, but must record on the custody record or in his pocket notebook the reasons for doing this.

C The officer cannot do this as the suspect is not a person detained under the Terrorism Act 2000.

D The officer cannot do this as no specific threat has been made against him.

Question 8.8

Constable VENISON was interviewing GOUDY who had been arrested the previous evening for an assault. During the interview, the recording equipment fails and attempts to use new recording media are not successful. There are no other recording facilities readily available.

What action should Constable VENISON now take?

A The interview will have to wait until recording facilities become available and the officer should note on the new media the reasons for the delay.

B The interview will have to wait until recording facilities become available and the officer should précis the original interview prior to proceeding with the new one.

C The interview may continue without being audibly recorded (it can be recorded in writing). If this happens, the interviewer shall seek the custody officer's authority.

D The interview may continue without being audibly recorded. If this happens, the interviewer shall seek the authority of an officer not below the rank of inspector.

Question 8.9

EDDISON has been arrested for an offence of theft and taken to a designated police station. Constable DAVIES is interviewing EDDISON (who is accompanied by his solicitor) using a removable recording media device at the designated police station. At the conclusion of the interview, the solicitor refuses to sign the master recording label although EDDISON does sign the label.

What action should Constable DAVIES now take?

A She should note the fact that the solicitor has refused to sign; no further action is required as the suspect did sign the label.

B The custody officer should be called into the interview room and asked to sign the label.

C An officer of at least the rank of inspector should be called into the interview room and asked to sign the label.

D Any officer of or above the rank of sergeant should be called into the interview room and asked to sign the label.

Question 8.10

DRURY has been arrested for a series of burglaries and has been in custody for some time and is being put into a rest period. After two hours, his solicitor arrives and requests an urgent consultation with his client.

In relation to this, which of the following is correct?

A As this is an urgent request, it should be allowed and after consultation a fresh eight-hour rest period should be given.

B Any request from a legal adviser should be granted and after consultation a fresh eight-hour rest period should be given.

C As this is an urgent request, it should be allowed and after consultation a fresh six-hour rest period should be given.

D Any request from a legal adviser should be granted and after consultation a fresh six-hour rest period should be given.

Question 8.11

Officers are about to interview YOUNG in relation to a robbery offence. The officers are also planning to hold an identification procedure later, after they have carried out this interview. They have a first description of the suspect that was obtained from a witness to the offence, and YOUNG is represented by a legal adviser.

Must the officers disclose this first description to the suspect and his solicitor?

A Yes, as they know an identification procedure will follow.

B Yes, but only if they intend asking him questions about this description.

C No, there is no requirement to provide the first description at this stage.

D No, a first description need only be supplied after an identification procedure is held.

Question 8.12

GODDARD has been arrested for murder and is represented at police interview by his legal adviser. The solicitor asks the police to provide the cause of death as part of their disclosure to him but the police refuse. He therefore advises his client to exercise his right to silence as he cannot properly advise his client as he does not know the cause of death.

Which of the following is correct in relation to adverse inferences that could be drawn due to this silence at interview?

A Inferences could be drawn as GODDARD must put forward a defence even where his solicitor advises silence.

B Inferences should not be drawn as the officers must disclose the cause of death.

C Inferences should not be drawn as the officers should give basic information, and the cause of death would be basic information.

D Inferences should not be drawn as GODDARD refused to answer questions on his solicitor's advice.

Question 8.13

Detective Constables McANGUS and LAPORTE are investigating a complex fraud case that has occurred over many years. As a result, they are carrying out a series of interviews and need to build breaks into their interview schedule.

How long should a meal break normally last?

A At least 30 minutes.

B At least 45 minutes.

C At least one hour.

D At least one hour 15 minutes.

Question 8.14

Constable CONWAY has arrested HOWE in relation to an offence of theft. The officer is interviewing HOWE regarding the offence at a designated police station and has gained a significant amount of evidence. Constable CONWAY has put all the questions he considers relevant to HOWE and has given HOWE an opportunity to give an innocent explanation for the circumstances he found himself in and is wondering at what point in time the interview should be concluded.

When should the officer conclude the interview?

A When the custody officer reasonably believes there is sufficient evidence to provide a realistic prospect of conviction.

B When the custody officer reasonably suspects there is sufficient evidence to prosecute.

C When the officer in charge of the investigation (Constable CONWAY) reasonably believes there is sufficient evidence to provide a realistic prospect of conviction.

D When the officer in charge of the investigation (Constable CONWAY) reasonably suspects there is sufficient evidence to prosecute.

Question 8.15

GREENING is suffering from a significant mental disorder but is suspected of being involved in a case where a young girl was kidnapped. The girl has not been found but GREENING has been arrested and an appropriate adult will not be available for at least two hours. Police officers wish to urgently interview GREENING as any consequent delay may lead to physical harm to the girl and the superintendent is considering the matter.

Which of the following is correct?

A GREENING can be interviewed provided his solicitor is present during the interview.

B GREENING can be interviewed provided the superintendent is satisfied that the interview would not significantly harm GREENING's physical or mental state.

C GREENING cannot be interviewed under any circumstances without an appropriate adult being present.

D GREENING cannot be interviewed unless a mental health professional agrees that it would not significantly harm his mental health.

Question 8.16

Constable DE MARCO is investigating an assault involving a wounding. The complainant states that WATERS had stabbed him in the arm with a knife in the street outside his house; WATERS then used the knife to cut his hand and rubbed this across the wound he had caused in the complainant's arm. WATERS said 'Now you have HIV as well as me'. The officer went to WATERS's address and arrested him, seizing a bloodstained knife. During the interview, WATERS stated that he had cut his hand whilst chopping an onion but said 'No comment' to questions about the knife.

In these circumstances, can a special warning under s. 36 of the Criminal Justice and Public Order Act 1994 be given?

A Yes, in relation to the cut on WATERS's hand and also the knife.

B Yes, in relation to the knife only.

C No, the knife was not 'found' at a place at or about the time the offence for which he was arrested is alleged to have been committed.

D No, the cut is not a 'mark' as defined in s. 36 and therefore not subject to a special warning.

Question 8.17

DICKENS makes a complaint to the police about a robbery. During the struggle, DICKENS states that he bit the perpetrator on the hand, enough to probably leave teeth marks. The police suspect FRENCH and arrest him in the street, and he has bite marks on his hand. A lawfully conducted search of his house finds items stolen from DICKENS. During interview, he refuses to answer questions about the property found in his house, and states that he was bitten by his girlfriend during sex.

What, if anything, can FRENCH be given a 'special warning' about (under s. 36 of the Criminal Justice and Public Order Act 1994)?

A The teeth marks only.

B The property found in his house only.

C The teeth marks and the property found in his house.

D The police cannot give a special warning for either the teeth marks or the property found.

Question 8.18

HARDEMAN (aged 13 years) has been arrested for burglary and is being interviewed regarding the offence by PCs GEORGE and WEBB. HARDEMAN's solicitor is present along with QUINTON who is HARDEMAN's uncle and is acting as an appropriate adult for HARDEMAN. During the interview, QUINTON becomes exceptionally and unreasonably obstructive, preventing proper questions being put to HARDEMAN by constantly answering questions on HARDEMAN's behalf.

According to Code C of the Codes of Practice, what action should be taken in these circumstances?

A The interviewer should stop the interview and consult the custody officer.

B The interviewer should stop the interview and consult an officer not below inspector rank, if one is readily available, not connected with the investigation. Otherwise the interviewer should consult the custody officer.

C The interviewer should stop the interview and consult an officer not below superintendent rank, if one is readily available, and otherwise an officer not below inspector rank not connected with the investigation.

D The interviewer should stop the interview and explain to the appropriate adult that if their obstructive behaviour continues they will be removed from the interview and another appropriate adult will be contacted to represent the interests of the detained juvenile.

Question 8.19

PS DREW and PC PRENTICE are interviewing TASKER in respect of a criminal damage matter. TASKER is legally represented by WARING in the interview. During the interview, TASKER asks if he can use the toilet and also requests a drink of water. PS DREW agrees to TASKER's requests, stops the interview and turns off the recording media recorder. TASKER states that he will only be a minute or two as he is escorted to the toilet by PC PRENTICE, leaving PS DREW and WARING in the interview room.

What should PS DREW do with regard to the recording media left in the recorder?

A When a break is taken and the interview room vacated by the suspect, the recording media shall be removed from the recorder and the procedures for the conclusion of an interview followed.

B When the break is a short one and the interviewer remains in the interview room, there is no need to remove the recording media. When the interview recommences, the recording should continue on the same recording media.

C As this is only a short break and the suspect's solicitor remains in the interview room with PS DREW, the recording media should remain in the recorder. The same recording media should be used when the interview recommences.

D Regardless of the length of the break or who remains in the interview room, the procedure for the conclusion of an interview should be followed and a new set of recording media should be used when the interview recommences.

Question 8.20

LYON has been arrested for an offence of robbery and on arrest states: 'I only did it because I was desperate for cash.' The arresting officer, PC VICKERY (a probationary officer), recorded the response in his pocket notebook. LYON is later interviewed by DC STONE (an officer with ten years' police service) and PC VICKERY. PC VICKERY follows the Codes of Practice in respect of the interview and, after cautioning LYON, he presents him with a copy of his pocket notebook containing the comment made after arrest and asks LYON to sign it. LYON examines the pocket notebook entry and states that he does not agree with the recorded comment, denying that he ever said the words. PC VICKERY records the disagreement and asks LYON to read the details and sign them to the effect that they accurately reflect his disagreement. LYON refuses to do so.

If the Codes of Practice are to be complied with, what should occur in respect of the refusal to sign by LYON?

A The senior police officer in the interview (DC STONE) must record LYON's refusal to sign the record of disagreement.

B The custody officer must be called into the interview to record LYON's refusal to sign the record of disagreement.

C An officer of the rank of inspector or above must be called into the interview room to record LYON's refusal to sign the record of disagreement.

D Either one of the officers present in the interview should record LYON's refusal to sign the record of the disagreement.

Question 8.21

FRANCIS has attended a police station for the purposes of a voluntary interview. It is alleged that FRANCIS has stolen £500 from a charity collection and PC ROCKELL (the investigating officer) is going to interview FRANCIS and ask questions about the allegation. Unfortunately, an authorised recording device in working order is not available, meaning that there is no viable alternative but to make a written record of the interview.

Which of the comments below is correct in respect of the 'relevant officer' in such a case?

A The 'relevant officer' will be an officer of the rank of inspector or above.

B The 'relevant officer' will be an officer of the rank of sergeant or above in consultation with the investigating officer.

C The 'relevant officer' will be a custody officer at the nearest designated police station.

D The 'relevant officer' will be PC ROCKELL.

Question 8.22

CONEY has been arrested for assault and is being interviewed by PS STYLES and PC PRICE; CONEY's solicitor, BOYLE, is present in the interview. At the conclusion of the interview, the recorder is switched off and PS STYLES seals the master recording media with a master recording label and both he and PC PRICE sign the label. CONEY also signs the label but BOYLE refuses to do so.

Which of the following statements is correct with regard to this situation?

A Either officer should make a note in their pocket notebooks that BOYLE refused to sign the label.

B An officer of at least the rank of inspector or, if one is not available, the custody officer, should be called into the interviewing room to sign the label.

C The senior officer in the interview should note in his/her pocket notebook the fact that BOYLE has refused to sign the label.

D The custody officer or another sergeant should be called into the interview room and asked to sign the master recording label.

ANSWERS

Answer 8.1

Answer **C** — PACE Code C, para. 10.1 states:

> A person whom there are grounds to suspect of an offence, must be cautioned before any questions about an offence, or further questions if the answers provide the grounds for suspicion, are put to them if either the suspect's answers or silence, (i.e. failure or refusal to answer or answer satisfactorily) may be given in evidence to a court in a prosecution. A person need not be cautioned if questions are for other necessary purposes, e.g.: (a) solely to establish their identity or ownership of any vehicle ...

So although there are grounds to suspect the vehicle is stolen (the ANPR report), what is vital is the officer's belief about the person he is about to question. Here the officer does not suspect the driver of stealing the car and therefore need not caution him; answers A and B are therefore incorrect.

Note that the Code states that a person need not be cautioned to establish ownership of a vehicle; however, that is not always clear-cut where the vehicle is stolen. In this scenario, had the officer suspected the driver of stealing the car then there would be grounds to suspect him of an offence and a caution must be given. Where such suspicion exists, questions about ownership form part of an interview about the offence and are subject to caution; answer D is therefore incorrect. Had the officer suspected that the driver was in possession of drugs then a caution to establish identity/ownership need not be given as those questions do not relate to the offence under suspicion.

Evidence and Procedure, para. 2.8.2

Answer 8.2

Answer **A** — At the beginning of an interview, the interviewer, after cautioning the suspect, shall put to him/her any significant statement or silence which occurred in the presence and hearing of a police officer or other police staff before the start of the interview and which have not been put to the suspect in the course of a previous interview. The interviewer shall ask the suspect whether he/she confirms or denies that earlier statement or silence and if he/she wants to add anything.

A significant statement is one which appears capable of being used in evidence against the suspect, in particular a direct admission of guilt.

Whether a joke or not, the statement made by the suspect would be capable of being given in evidence against him/her even though it was not a direct admission of guilt; answer D is therefore incorrect.

The statement can be made anywhere (not just a police station) and can be said to police staff as well as police officers; answers B and C are therefore incorrect.

Evidence and Procedure, para. 2.8.3

Answer 8.3

Answer **D** — Interviews at educational establishments should take place only in exceptional circumstances and with the agreement of the head teacher or the head teacher's nominee (PACE Code C, para. 11.16). This is the mandatory practice; however, it is not mandatory that the head teacher be the appropriate adult, and therefore answer A is incorrect. If waiting for the parents (or other appropriate adult) to attend would cause unreasonable delay, the head teacher can be the appropriate adult, and this is not dependent on the parents' consent and therefore answer C is incorrect. The only exception to this is where the juvenile is suspected of an offence against his/her educational establishment, as the youth is in the question. In these circumstances, the head teacher cannot be the appropriate adult and answer B is therefore incorrect (Code C, para. 11.16).

Evidence and Procedure, para. 2.8.3.2

Answer 8.4

Answer **C** — Answer C provides the correct procedure to be followed in this situation. If the suspect, or an appropriate adult on their behalf, objects to the interview being audibly recorded either at the outset, during the interview or during a break, the interviewer shall explain that the interview is being audibly recorded and that this Code requires the objections to be recorded on the audio recording. When any objections have been audibly recorded or the suspect or appropriate adult has refused to have his/her objections recorded, the relevant officer shall decide in accordance with para. 2.3(d) (which requires the officer to have regard to the nature and circumstances of the objections) whether a written record of the interview or its continuation is to be made and that audio recording should be turned off. Following a decision that a written record is to be made, the interviewer shall say they are turning off the recorder and shall then make a written record of the interview as in Code C, section 11. If, however, following a decision that a written record is not to be made, the interviewer may proceed to question the suspect with the audio recording still on. The 'relevant officer' in this situation will be the custody officer (see Code E, para. 2.4).

Evidence and Procedure, paras 2.8.8 to 2.8.9

Answer 8.5

Answer **B** — Code C, para. 11.2 states:

> Immediately prior to the commencement or re-commencement of any interview at a police station or other authorised place of detention, the interviewer should remind the suspect of their entitlement to free legal advice and that the interview can be delayed for legal advice to be obtained, unless one of the exceptions in paragraph 6.6 applies.

After any break in questioning under caution, the person being questioned must be made aware that they remain under caution. If there is any doubt, the relevant caution should be given again in full when the interview resumes (also see Code E, para. 3.16 for emphasis of this point).

The requirement is to remind the suspect and caution again only where there is doubt about whether the suspect knows they are still under caution; answers A and C are therefore incorrect. The fact the suspect is legally represented does not change this; answer D is therefore incorrect.

Evidence and Procedure, paras 2.8.3, 2.8.9

Answer 8.6

Answer **A** — It is important not to confuse the duty of disclosure to a person once charged with the need to disclose evidence to a suspect before interviewing them. After a person has been charged, and before trial, the rules of disclosure are clear and almost all relevant material must be disclosed to the defence.

However, this is not necessarily the case at the interview stage of the investigation. There is no specific provision within PACE for the disclosure of any information by the police at the police station, *with the exception of the custody record*. In respect of the provision of a copy of the 'first description' of a suspect, it should be noted that Code D (para. 3.1) states that a copy of the 'first description' shall, where practicable, be given to the suspect or his/her solicitor before any procedures under paras 3.5 to 3.10, 3.21 or 3.23 are carried out. In other words, the disclosure requirement is that a copy of the 'first description' shall, where practicable, be given to the suspect or his/her solicitor *before a video identification, an identification parade, a group identification or confrontation takes place*. Therefore, an officer disclosing information to a solicitor at the interview stage (which is taking place in advance of any identification procedures), need not provide the 'first description' of a suspect at that time.

Further, there is nothing within the Criminal Justice and Public Order Act 1994 that states that information must be disclosed before an inference from silence can be made. Indeed, in *R v Imran* [1997] Crim LR 754 the court held that it is totally wrong to submit that a defendant should be prevented from lying by being presented with the whole of the evidence against him/her prior to the interview.

So at this stage only the custody record is required to be disclosed; answers B, C and D are therefore incorrect.

Evidence and Procedure, para. 2.8.4.3

Answer 8.7

Answer **B** — Nothing in PACE Code E or F requires the identity of an officer to be recorded or disclosed if the interviewer reasonably believes that recording or disclosing his/her name might put him/her in danger.

This is not restricted to terrorism offences; answer C is therefore incorrect.

Note that there is no need for a specific threat to be made against a particular officer; answer D is therefore incorrect.

In such a case, the officer should use his/her warrant or other identification number and the name of the police station to which he/she is attached. The officer may have his/her back to the visual recording device (Code E, para. 2.7(a)). Such instances and the reasons for them shall be recorded in the custody record or the interviewer's pocket notebook; answer A is therefore incorrect.

Evidence and Procedure, paras 2.8.7, 2.8.13

Answer 8.8

Answer **C** — If there is an equipment failure which can be rectified quickly, e.g. by inserting new recording media, the interviewer shall follow the appropriate procedures as in para. 3.12. When the recording is resumed, the interviewer shall explain what happened and record the time the interview recommences. However, if it is not possible to continue recording using the same recording device or by using a replacement device, the interview should be audio recorded using a secure digital recording network device if the necessary equipment is available. If it is not available, the interview may continue and be recorded in writing (answers A and B are therefore incorrect) as directed by the 'relevant officer' (in this case the custody officer, not an inspector—answer D is incorrect).

Evidence and Procedure, para. 2.8.9

Answer 8.9

Answer **C** — At the conclusion of the interview, including the taking and reading back of any written statement, the time shall be recorded and the recording shall be stopped. The interviewer shall seal the master recording with a master recording label and treat it as an exhibit in accordance with force standing orders. The interviewer shall sign the label and ask the suspect and any third party present during the interview to sign it. If the suspect or third party refuses to sign the label, an officer *of at least the rank of inspector* (making answers A, B and D incorrect), or if not available the custody officer, or if the suspect has not been arrested, a sergeant, shall be called into the interview room and asked to sign it.

Evidence and Procedure, para. 2.8.9

Answer 8.10

Answer **D** — PACE Code C, para. 12.2 provides that a detained person must have a continuous eight-hour 'rest period' while he/she is in detention; this period should normally be at night. The period should be free from questioning, travel or any interruption by police officers in connection with the case. The period may not be interrupted or delayed, except:

(a) when there are reasonable grounds for believing not delaying or interrupting the period would:
  (i) involve a risk of harm to people or serious loss of, or damage to, property;
  (ii) delay unnecessarily the person's release from custody;
  (iii) otherwise prejudice the outcome of the investigation;
(b) at the request of the detainee, their appropriate adult or legal representative [this relates to any request not just those that are urgent; answers A and C are therefore incorrect];
(c) when a delay or interruption is necessary in order to:
  (i) comply with the legal obligations and duties arising under s. 15;
  (ii) take action required under s. 9 or in accordance with medical advice.

If the period is interrupted in accordance with (a), a fresh period must be allowed.

Interruptions under (b) and (c) do not require a fresh period to be allowed. The question relates to point (b) and therefore having had two hours' rest before being interrupted, six more are allocated; answer B is therefore incorrect.

Evidence and Procedure, para. 2.8.4

Answer 8.11

Answer **C** — There is no specific provision within the Police and Criminal Evidence Act 1984 or the Codes of Practice for the disclosure of any information by the police at the police station, with the exception of the custody record and, generally in identification procedures, the initial description given by the witnesses. In respect of the provision of a copy of the 'first description' of a suspect, it should be noted that Code D (para. 3.1) states that a copy of the 'first description' shall, where practicable, be given to the suspect or his/her solicitor before any procedures under paras 3.5 to 3.10, 3.21 or 3.23 are carried out. In other words, the disclosure requirement is that a copy of the 'first description' shall, where practicable, be given to the suspect or his/her solicitor before a video identification, an identification parade, a group identification or confrontation takes place. Therefore, an officer disclosing information to a solicitor at the interview stage (which is taking place in advance of any identification procedures) need not provide the 'first description' of a suspect at that time; answers A, B and D are therefore incorrect.

Evidence and Procedure, para. 2.8.4.3

Answer 8.12

Answer **A** — There is nothing within the Criminal Justice and Public Order Act 1994 that states that information must be disclosed by the police prior to interview before an inference from silence can be made; answer B is therefore incorrect. Indeed, in *R v Imran* [1997] Crim LR 754 the court held that it is totally wrong to submit that a defendant should be prevented from lying by being presented with the whole of the evidence against him/her prior to the interview. In *R v Hoare* [2004] EWCA Crim 784, the Court of Appeal held that the purpose of s. 34 was to qualify a defendant's right to silence rather than to exclude a jury from drawing an adverse inference against a defendant merely because he/she had been advised by his/her solicitor to remain silent, whether or not he/she genuinely or reasonably relied on that advice. Where a defendant had an explanation to give that was consistent with his/her innocence, it was not 'reasonable', within the meaning of s. 34(1), for him/her to fail to give that explanation in interview even where he/she had been advised by his/her solicitor to remain silent. Legal advice by itself could not preclude the drawing of an adverse inference; answer D is therefore incorrect. There is a balance to be struck between providing the solicitor with enough information to understand the nature of the case against his/her client and keeping back material which, if disclosed, may allow the suspect the opportunity to avoid implicating him/herself. For instance, in *R v Thirlwell* [2002] EWCA Crim 286 the Court of Appeal agreed that the solicitor had not been entitled to provisional medical evidence as to possible causes of death in a murder case; answer C is therefore incorrect.

Evidence and Procedure, para. 2.8.4.3

Answer 8.13

Answer **B** — Meal breaks should normally last at least 45 minutes and shorter breaks after two hours should last at least 15 minutes; answers A, C and D are therefore incorrect.

Evidence and Procedure, para. 2.8.4.1

Answer 8.14

Answer **A** — The interview or further interview of a person about an offence with which that person has not been charged or for which he/she has not been informed he/she may be prosecuted, must cease when:

(a) the officer in charge of the investigation is satisfied all the questions they consider relevant to obtaining accurate and reliable information about the offence have been put to the suspect, this includes allowing the suspect an opportunity to give an innocent explanation and asking questions to test if the explanation is accurate and reliable, e.g. to clear up ambiguities or clarify what the suspect said;

(b) the officer in charge of the investigation has taken account of any other available evidence; and

(c) the officer in charge of the investigation, or in the case of a detained suspect, the custody officer, reasonably believes there is sufficient evidence to provide a realistic prospect of conviction for that offence.

As HOWE is in detention, the decision at (c) will be made by the custody officer (eliminating answers C and D). It is a reasonable *belief* (not suspicion) so answer B is incorrect.

Evidence and Procedure, para. 2.8.3

Answer 8.15

Answer **B** — Code C states that a juvenile or person who is mentally disordered or otherwise mentally vulnerable must not be interviewed regarding his/her involvement or suspected involvement in a criminal offence or offences, or asked to provide or sign a written statement under caution or record of interview, in the absence of the appropriate adult, unless paras 11.1, 11.18 to 11.20 apply; answer C is therefore incorrect. Paragraph 11.1 outlines that where there was a risk of physical harm to a person, an interview without an appropriate adult may take place; this is not dependent on the suspect's solicitor being present—answer A is therefore incorrect. The interview can only take place where a police officer of at least the rank of superintendent considers that delay will lead to the consequences in para. 11.1(a) to (c), and is satisfied that the interview would not significantly harm the person's physical or mental state. No mental health professional's advice is needed; answer D is therefore incorrect.

Evidence and Procedure, para. 2.8.3.2

Answer 8.16

Answer **B** — Section 36 of the Criminal Justice and Public Order Act 1994 provides that inferences can be drawn from an accused's failure to give evidence or refusal to answer any question about any object, substance or mark which may be attributable to the accused in the commission of an offence.

Section 36 states:

(1) Where—
  (a) a person is arrested by a constable, and there is—
    (i)   on his person; or
    (ii) in or on his clothing or footwear; or
    (iii) otherwise in his possession; or
    (iv) in any place in which he is at the time of his arrest,
    any object, substance or mark, or there is any mark on any such object; and
  (b) that or another constable investigating the case reasonably believes that the presence of the object, substance or mark may be attributable to the participation of the person arrested in the commission of an offence specified by the constable; and
  (c) the constable informs the person arrested that he so believes, and requests him to account for the presence of the object, substance or mark; and
  (d) the person fails or refuses to do so...

In this scenario, the cut would be a mark on his person; as mark is not defined in the legislation this could be 'any' mark; answer D is therefore incorrect. However, since the suspect has in fact accounted for that mark in accordance with s. 36(1)(c) of the 1994 Act, it could not be the subject of a special warning (whether you actually believe the account or not is irrelevant); answer A is therefore incorrect.

'Found by him at a place at or about the time the offence for which he was arrested is alleged to have been committed' relates to the person being found as in s. 37 of the Criminal Justice and Public Order Act 1994, not s. 36. Section 36 considers the circumstances of the suspect at the time of arrest; it is suggested, therefore, that in relation to items that are otherwise in the possession of the suspect under s. 36(1)(a), there must be some link to the suspect at the time of arrest and this would not, for instance, include items found some time later at a search of the suspect's home address some distance away. What is important in s. 36 is what is found in the place where the person is at the time of his/her arrest, in this case the knife; answer C is therefore incorrect.

Evidence and Procedure, para. 2.8.2.5

Answer 8.17

Answer **D** — Section 36 of the Criminal Justice and Public Order Act 1994 provides that inferences can be drawn from an accused's failure to give evidence or refusal to answer any question about any object, substance or mark which may be attributable to the accused in the commission of an offence.

Section 36 states:

(1) Where—
  (a) a person is arrested by a constable, and there is—
    (i)   on his person; or
    (ii) in or on his clothing or footwear; or
    (iii) otherwise in his possession; or
    (iv) in any place in which he is at the time of his arrest, any object, substance or mark, or there is any mark on any such object; and
  (b) that or another constable investigating the case reasonably believes that the presence of the object, substance or mark may be attributable to the participation of the person arrested in the commission of an offence specified by the constable; and
  (c) the constable informs the person arrested that he so believes, and requests him to account for the presence of the object, substance or mark; and
  (d) the person fails or refuses to do so...

The teeth marks are definitely on his person; however, he did account for the mark (its believability is irrelevant) and as such he cannot be given a special warning for it; answers A and C are therefore incorrect.

The property was not found on his person or in the place where he was arrested, so it also cannot be subject to a special warning, even if he refuses to account for that property; answers B and C are therefore incorrect.

Evidence and Procedure, para. 2.8.2.5

Answer 8.18

Answer **C** — Code C, para. 11.17A states that the appropriate adult may be required to leave the interview if their conduct is such that the interviewer is unable properly to put questions to the suspect. This will include situations where the appropriate adult's approach or conduct prevents or unreasonably obstructs proper questions being put to the suspect or the suspect's responses being recorded. If the interviewer considers an appropriate adult is acting in such a way, he/she will stop the interview and consult an officer not below superintendent rank, if one is readily available, and otherwise an officer not below inspector rank not connected with the investigation. After speaking to the appropriate adult, the officer consulted must remind the adult that their role under para. 11.17 does not allow him/her to obstruct proper questioning and give the adult an opportunity to respond. The officer consulted will then decide if the interview should continue without the attendance of that appropriate adult. If the officer decides that it should, another appropriate adult must be obtained before the interview continues, unless the provisions of para. 11.18 apply. Answers A, B and D are therefore incorrect.

Evidence and Procedure, para. 2.8.3.2

Answer 8.19

Answer **A** — If the suspect leaves the interview room during a break, then the recording media shall be removed from the recorder and the procedures for the conclusion of an interview followed. If the suspect leaves the interview room, then it is immaterial whether an interviewer or solicitor or both remain, making answers B and C incorrect. If the suspect remains in the interview room during the short break, there is no need to remove the recording media and the same recording media can be used when the interview recommences, making answer D incorrect (Code E, paras 3.13 to 3.16).

Evidence and Procedure, para. 2.8.9

Answer 8.20

Answer **D** — Significant statements described in paras 11.4 and 11.4A of Code C (the comment made by LYON on arrest) will always be relevant to the offence and must be recorded. When a suspect agrees to read records of interviews and other comments and sign them as correct, he/she should be asked to endorse the record with, for example, 'I agree that this is a correct record of what was said' and add his/her signature. If the suspect does not agree with the record, the interviewer should record the details of any disagreement and ask the suspect to read those details and sign them to the effect that they accurately reflect his/her disagreement. Any refusal to sign should be recorded. Answers A, B and C are therefore incorrect.

Evidence and Procedure, para. 2.8.3.1

Answer 8.21

Answer **B** — In the case of a voluntary interview which takes place at a police station and the offence in question is an indictable offence (theft under s. 1(1) of the Theft Act 1968 is an indictable offence), the 'relevant officer' means an officer of the rank of sergeant or above in consultation with the investigating officer, meaning that answers A, C and D are incorrect.

Evidence and Procedure, para. 2.8.8

Answer 8.22

Answer **B** — If a suspect or a third party refuses to sign the label, an officer of at least the rank of inspector or, if one is not available, the custody officer or, if the suspect has not been arrested, a sergeant, shall be called into the interview room and asked to sign the label (Code E, para. 3.20). Answer A, C and D are therefore incorrect.

Evidence and Procedure, para. 2.8.9

Question Checklist

The following checklist is designed to help you keep track of your progress when answering the multiple choice questions. If you fill this in after one attempt at each question, you will be able to check how many you have got right and which questions you need to revisit a second time. Also available online; to download visit www.blackstonespoliceservice.com.

	First attempt Correct (✓)	Second attempt Correct (✓)
1 Instituting Criminal Proceedings		
1.1		
1.2		
1.3		
1.4		
1.5		
1.6		
1.7		
1.8		
1.9		
1.10		

	First attempt Correct (✓)	Second attempt Correct (✓)
2 Release of Person Arrested		
2.1		
2.2		
2.3		
2.4		
2.5		
2.6		
2.7		
2.8		
2.9		
2.10		

Question Checklist

	First attempt Correct (✓)	Second attempt Correct (✓)
2.11		
2.12		
2.13		
2.14		
2.15		
2.16		
2.17		
2.18		
2.19		
2.20		
2.21		
2.22		
2.23		
2.24		
3 Court Procedure and Witnesses		
3.1		
3.2		
3.3		
3.4		
3.5		
3.6		
3.7		
3.8		
3.9		
3.10		

	First attempt Correct (✓)	Second attempt Correct (✓)
3.11		
3.12		
3.13		
4 Exclusion of Admissible Evidence		
4.1		
4.2		
4.3		
4.4		
4.5		
4.6		
4.7		
4.8		
4.9		
4.10		
5 Disclosure of Evidence		
5.1		
5.2		
5.3		
5.4		
5.5		
5.6		
5.7		
5.8		
5.9		
5.10		
5.11		
5.12		

	First attempt Correct (✓)	Second attempt Correct (✓)
6 Detention and Treatment of Persons by Police Officers		
6.1		
6.2		
6.3		
6.4		
6.5		
6.6		
6.7		
6.8		
6.9		
6.10		
6.11		
6.12		
6.13		
6.14		
6.15		
6.16		
6.17		
6.18		
6.19		
6.20		
6.21		
6.22		
6.23		
6.24		
6.25		

	First attempt Correct (✓)	Second attempt Correct (✓)
6.26		
6.27		
6.28		
6.29		
6.30		
6.31		
6.32		
6.33		
6.34		
6.35		
6.36		
6.37		
6.38		
6.39		
6.40		
7 Identification		
7.1		
7.2		
7.3		
7.4		
7.5		
7.6		
7.7		
7.8		
7.9		
7.10		
7.11		

	First attempt Correct (✓)	Second attempt Correct (✓)
7.12		
7.13		
7.14		
7.15		
7.16		
7.17		
7.18		
7.19		
7.20		
8 Interviews		
8.1		
8.2		
8.3		
8.4		
8.5		
8.6		

	First attempt Correct (✓)	Second attempt Correct (✓)
8.7		
8.8		
8.9		
8.10		
8.11		
8.12		
8.13		
8.14		
8.15		
8.16		
8.17		
8.18		
8.19		
8.20		
8.21		
8.22